General editor: Graham Han

Brodie's Notes on Dylan Thomas's
Under Milk Wood

J. S. Dugdale MA

MACMILLAN

The excerpts from *Under Milk Wood* are reprinted
by kind permission of J. M. Dent & Sons Ltd
and the Trustees for the Copyrights of the late Dylan Thomas

© J. S. Dugdale 1964, 1976, 1992

First published 1964 by James Brodie Ltd
Published 1976 by Pan Books Ltd

This revised edition published 1992 by
MACMILLAN PRESS LTD
Houndmills, Basingstoke, Hampshire RG21 6XS
and London
Companies and representatives
throughout the world

ISBN 0–333–58208–X

A catalogue record for this book is available
from the British Library.

This book is printed on paper suitable for recycling and
made from fully managed and sustained forest sources.

10   9   8   7   6   5   4   3   2
04   03   02   01   00   99   98   97   96

Printed in Great Britain by
Mackays of Chatham PLC
Chatham, Kent

Contents

To the student

A close reading of the set text is the student's primary task. These Notes will help to increase your understanding and appreciation of the play, and to stimulate *your own* thinking about it: *they are in no way intended as a substitute* for a thorough knowledge of the play.

Preface by the general editor

The intention throughout this study aid is to stimulate and
guide, to encourage your involvement in the book, and to
develop informed responses and a sure understanding of the
main details.

Brodie's Notes provide a clear outline of the play or novel's
plot, followed by act, scene, or chapter summaries and/or
commentaries. These are designed to emphasize the most
important literary and factual details. Poems, stories or non-
fiction texts combine brief summary with critical commentary
on individual aspects or common features of the genre being
examined. Textual notes define what is difficult or obscure
and emphasize literary qualities. Revision questions are set at
appropriate points to test your ability to appreciate the prescribed book and to write accurately and relevantly about it.

In addition, each of these Notes includes a critical appreciation of the author's art. This covers such major elements as
characterization, style, structure, setting and themes. Poems
are examined technically – rhyme, rhythm, for instance. In
fact, any important aspect of the prescribed work will be
evaluated. The aim is to send you back to the text you are
studying.

Each study aid concludes with a series of general questions
which require a detailed knowledge of the book: some of these
questions may invite comparison with other books, some will
be suitable for coursework exercises, and some could be
adapted to work you are doing on another book or books.
Each study aid has been adapted to meet the needs of the
current examination requirements. They provide a basic, individual and imaginative response to the work being studied,
and it is hoped that they will stimulate you to acquire dis-
ciplined reading habits and critical fluency.

Graham Handley 1992

The author

1 His life and work 1914–39

Dylan Thomas (1914–53) first appeared on the literary scene in 1934 with a opuscule simply entitled *18 Poems*; he died some twenty years later when he was thirty-nine years old. During the whole of this period he had been rated highly for at least a handful of his poems and, in general, had a considerable reputation. The height of his fame was reached when his *Collected Poems 1934–52* was published in 1952. Over 10,000 copies of this book were sold even before his death, an astronomical figure in the world of poetry-publishing today. Undoubtedly Augustus John's portrait of him as a young man – the curly hair, the nervously dilating nostrils, the visionary eyes – helped to endear him to the public: he corresponded to the popular conception of what a poet should look like.

Vernon Watkins has described his first meeting with the poet. 'He was slight, shorter than I had expected, shy, rather flushed and eager in manner, deep-voiced, restless, humorous, with large, wondering, yet acutely intelligent eyes, gold curls, snub-nose and the face of a cherub.' Dylan Thomas became great friends with Vernon Watkins and used to send the latter his poems more or less as he finished them. The *Letters* which Watkins managed to preserve must certainly be read as affording insight into the mind and personality of the poet. The effect he had on Americans during visits to the USA was similar to that he had on his friends in England. 'More of us loved than hated the irresponsible, charming, outrageous man; for he was our bourgeois idea of what a poet should be' (W. York Tindall, *A Reader's Guide to Dylan Thomas*, p. 12). People particularly liked his voice – not what he said, but how he said it: 'No triumph here of sense but of tone. Whether on academic stages, on gramophone records, or broadcast through the air, this voice, we knew, was the voice of true feeling.' It was inevitable that such a poet with such a voice would both please and displease. 'England was crowded with heavy dragoons, for whom the trouble with Thomas was that he came from the lower middle class. His father was a schoolteacher. Thomas wore no old school tie, his upper lip was far from stiff, and everything about him seemed too much. In short, he was a slob' (Tindall).

Thomas quickly became a kind of legend. 'He corresponded as most poets do not, to some popular ideal, vision, or fiction of what a poet, in real life, should be. He was the pattern of the poet as a bohemian, and this was in many ways a misfortune for him. Had he been a more aloof, a less gregarious, a more prudent man; had he been less ready to expend himself in casual sociability; had he had less of a knack, in his later years, for earning money quickly and spending it even more quickly; in any of these cases he might have lived longer and produced more; but he would not have been, in any of these cases, the writer that he is' (G. S. Fraser, *Dylan Thomas*, p. 1). As Fraser points out, Thomas achieves popularity in spite of the fact that many of his poems are, at least on the intellectual plane, almost incomprehensible (some critics would say, of certain poems, *wholly* incomprehensible): the reason for his popularity might have been that he is 'one of the few modern poets who can be read aloud to a large, mixed audience with confidence in his going down. There is a massive emotional directness in his poems that at once comes across. At the heart of his poetry there is a baffling simplicity.' And Cecil Price, referring to Thomas's visit to the University College of Wales to address a student audience, says, 'For Dylan Thomas, words were full of witchery. His poetry was incantation, a charm to rob evil and good of their influences and leave us all *naked things of sense*. His voice was the supple instrument; it communicated the splendour, terror and simplicity of the world' (*Dylan Thomas: The Legend and the Poet*, p. 19).

Dylan Thomas was born of Welsh parents in October 1914, in Swansea, the son of a schoolmaster – a teacher of English, 'revered by his pupils for possessing the secret power of making them love and enjoy what he taught them' (Susan Rousillat). This is perhaps significant. There is little evidence of the effect his father had upon him or upon his literary development, but at least one can assert that he was brought up in an atmosphere of books. Although Dylan Thomas was not academically outstanding, we learn that he was good at English, was enthusiastic about amateur dramatics and the Reading and Debating Societies, and contributed 'neat and conventional poems', stories and parodies of modern poets to the school magazine. He probably disappointed his father by not working hard for a scholarship to the University, but his interests lay elsewhere. In six years at school he had turned out twenty-six poems, and in these and other literary efforts some of his future qualities as poet and story-teller are already evinced: 'A certain morbidity, a sprinkling sense of humour, and a liking for cascades of alliterative sounds. . . . His child-hood and school-days made him familiar with the Welsh Nonconformist creeds and rites, to which he probably owed his thorough knowledge of the Bible, from which later he was to borrow many symbols. The Bible was certainly the only book which could be said to have contributed to his intellec-tual formation. As a schoolboy he was more attracted by *direct visions and sensations* received from the outside world than by the *second-hand and dead revelations found in books'* (S. Rousillat).

As Susan Rousillat points out, interesting discoveries are to be made if one walks in the districts of Swansea where Dylan Thomas was brought up. She refers to 'the unique position of the school', which was 'built half-way on the slope of Town Hill and opened its windows upon Swansea Bay'. The immen-sity of sea and sky in the blurred distance gives an impression of infinity probably perceived by the sensitive and dreamy Dylan Thomas. . . . Are these vistas of an ever-recurring sea as a distant background responsible for the sea imagery so rich in Dylan Thomas's poetry?' (*Dylan Thomas: The Legend and the Poet*, p. 6).

Daniel Jones, in the symposium from which I have just quoted, also gives interesting details of Dylan Thomas's school-boy days. There was considerable literary activity, including collaboration on both prose and poetry. The two young collaborators had word obsessions – 'everything at one time was "little" or "white"; and sometimes an adjective became irresistibly funny in almost any connection; "innumerable bananas", "wilful moccasin", "a certain Mrs Prothero". These word games, and even the most facetious of our col-laborations, had a serious experimental purpose, and there is no doubt that they played an important part in Dylan's early poetic development' (op. cit., p. 17). Daniel Jones informs us that Dylan Thomas's early poems were simple lyrics, but in ten years they had changed into the violent imagery seen in the poems first printed in the *Sunday Referee*; during this period the poet underwent many influences, including early Yeats, Aldington, Sacheverell Sitwell and D. H. Lawrence, in that order.

His main interest at school, it seems, was editing the school magazine and writing most of it, 'but school subjects were

treated by him with disdain. This was consistent; at that time,
and throughout his life, Dylan Thomas hated the academic.
But in those early years his antipathy had less discrimination;
it was directed not only against the fossils but against much
that was significantly alive as well, if he happened to find for it
an academic association. For this reason, perhaps, his enthusi-
asm was limited almost wholly to contemporary verse; poets
of the school textbook were suspect, and for the time being he
kept them at arm's length. Passionately absorbed in language,
he had no interest in languages, preferring to take whatever
might trickle through the translator's sieve' (op. cit., pp. 17–
18). It is interesting to note what stress Daniel Jones gives to
Dylan Thomas's interest in language as such. 'In these early
years, words occupied Dylan's mind to the exclusion even of
things with which they have some connection: to him, the
cushat* and the ring-dove were as different as the ostrich and
the humming-bird' (op. cit., p. 18).

Mention has already been made of the seminal influence
of the Bible, and Cecil Price has reminded us that Dylan
Thomas's grandfather was a Welsh preacher. Cecil Price regards this as 'an important fact, explaining what he revolted
against and what he loved. In Wales the preacher is associated with a puritanical outlook, a code that Thomas *mocked
and feared*. The preacher is also the man of eloquence, filled
with the rapture of words. The tones of his voice are so
carefully matched with the ideas he suggests that his audience
is lifted out of itself, captured, and yet, at the same time,
feeling aesthetically aware of the beauty of the performance'
(op. cit., p. 19). This verbal excitement and transformation of
the personality is known in Welsh as the *hwyl* (Shakespeare's
poet with his eyes 'rolling in a fine frenzy' suggests one element of it) and the *hwyl* often descended on Dylan Thomas
when he was reciting or incanting his poems. 'In them was a
wild exultation, a singing note, a variation of effect from
phrase to phrase. It was evident that he was a man who cared
for words with a religious intensity. By the time he read the
last poem in his selection, there was in the audience that
curious crackling atmosphere that can be raised in Wales only
by words and hymns' (op. cit., p. 20).

Dylan Thomas had no interest in the academic life which

* The *cushat* is the ring-dove or wood-pigeon, but for Dylan Thomas the word evoked
a different entity.

his father would have preferred him to follow. It is obvious, however, from his poem to his old and infirm father ('Do not go Gentle into that Good Night', *Collected Poems*, p. 116) that he held the old man in great esteem:

And you, my father, there on the sad height
Curse, bless, me now with your fierce tears, I pray.

Dylan left school in 1931 at the age of seventeen, and for a short time worked on the Swansea weekly newspaper, the *Herald of Wales*. It seems that, although Wales was plunged in industrial depression, the poet was not interested in economic, social or political problems. Yet he had to find some means of at least partial self-support, and this job on the newspaper was 'a job which must have combined for him the appeal of bohemianism with that of the outer verges of literature' (G. Fraser, *Dylan Thomas*, p. 8). One of his tasks was to write critical articles on local poetry. It was, on the whole, an unsatisfactory and frustrating job and Dylan Thomas began to think of leaving Wales. (Some aspects of his life in Swansea can be read in his *Portrait of the Artist as a Young Dog*.) In an address to a Scottish Society of Writers in Edinburgh he said, 'I am a Welshman who does not live in his own country, mainly because he still wants to eat and drink, be rigged and roofed, and no Welsh writer can hunt his bread and butter in Wales today unless he pulls his forelock to the *Western Mail*, Bethesdas on Sunday, and enters public houses by the back door . . .'.

Dylan Thomas's first job then was that of a reviewer. As already stated, he was not a bookish person. Throughout his life his reading was desultory. In a letter to Vernon Watkins (October 1937) he says that he has read 'two dozen thrillers, the whole of the Jane Austen, some old Powys, a book of Turgenev, 3 lines by Gertrude Stein, and an anthology of Pure Poetry by George Moore. There are only about 2,000 books left in the house.' In another letter, written a month later, he says, 'I have brought nothing with me but a few Penguin Shakespeares and a pocket dictionary'. In spite of this lack of an academic background, his literary criticism was both subtle and incisive, as can be seen from several examples in his letters.

Dylan Thomas did not speak Welsh, though undoubtedly he knew odd words and phrases. Nor did he subscribe to the tenets of Welsh nationalism. Nevertheless, as Fraser insists, 'Wales remained to him home' and his Welshness was an important part of his make-up.

His first 'public' appearance as a poet was when he contributed to, and won prizes from, the poetry page of the *Sunday Referee*, a newspaper which financed the publication of his first collection of *18 Poems* in 1934. It was the 'Poet's Corner' of the *Sunday Referee* which started him on his career and made him leave Wales for London. His early experiences in London stimulated him to further efforts, and two years later, in 1936, appeared a second collection, *Twenty Five Poems*, which had been published individually in such reviews as *New Verse*, *John O'London's Weekly* and *Contemporary Prose and Poetry*. Public attention was drawn to him by the famous eulogy of Dame Edith Sitwell which appeared in the *Sunday Times*, 'Here alone, among the poets of the younger generation, is one who could produce sonnets worthy of our great heritage'. Three years later – just before the start of World War II, *The Map of Love* was published; it contained poems which he had written in the previous two years, as well as short stories which he had written before 1934. He was now twenty-five years old. Vernon Watkins informs us that Dylan liked the poems of his second volume, for the most part, much more than those of *18 Poems*, but some of the poems of the second volume were contemporary with those of *18 Poems*, and some were even earlier. Edith Sitwell had already in the *London Mercury* (February 1936) praised one of the poems, 'A Grief Ago' (*Collected Poems*, pp. 54–5). Edith Sitwell called the poem 'a miraculous concentration', and 'a beautiful poem'. She deplored its obscurities, but admired its internal sounds and the fugitive pattern of terminal dissonance, assonance and rhyme. It is interesting to observe that Vernon Watkins tried to persuade Dylan to omit two poems ('Now', and 'How Soon the Servant Sun' – *Collected Poems*, pp. 51–2 and 56–7) from *Twenty Five Poems*, as presenting 'a face of unwarrantable obscurity'. Dylan, however, did not wish to leave them out; the one poem which he hesitated to include was one which subsequently became very well-known, 'And Death Shall Have no Dominion'.

All the poems for *The Map of Love* were typed by Vernon Watkins, who became Dylan's best friend and mentor. Watkins informs us that Dylan greatly admired Years, whom he regarded as the greatest living poet, but that Thomas Hardy was his favourite poet of the century. He disliked the 'socio-logical poetry' of the nineteen-thirties. One reason for the warm friendship between Vernon Watkins and Dylan Thomas was perhaps, as Watkins says, that they were both 'religious poets' and neither of them had 'any aptitude for political reform'.* There were deep affinities between the two poets; 'His poems', says Watkins, 'spoke to me with the voice of metaphysical truth; if we disagreed it was on a metaphysical issue, for natural observation in poetry meant nothing to us without the support of metaphysical truth.'

The earliest letter to Vernon Watkins dates from April 1936, when Dylan was in Penzance. Already there is the recognizable impress of his personality and he tells Watkins, 'I am not a country man; I stand for, if anything, the aspidistra, the provincial drive, the morning café, the evening pub ...' (*Letters*, p. 23). He refers in this letter to his life in London ('Life No. 13'), which he characterizes as one of 'promiscuity, booze, coloured shirts, too much talk, too little work and nights out with Porteous, Cameron, Blakeston, Grigson and William Empson'. Life No. 13 in London was one of 'head-ache, liver and general seediness' (*Letters*, p. 24). He was living near Penzance 'in a cottage in a field', with 'my hostess or what you like', who psychoanalysed him over breakfast. Apparently he worked hard here, and expressed a fear, not of 'any sudden cessation or drying-up' but 'an ingrowing, the impulse growing like a toenail into the artifice'. Dylan is already in financial difficulties – as he is to remain throughout most of his life – and asks Watkins in a touching postscript to lend him a pound or two.

The next letter is dated July 1937, and this time comes from Mousehole. Three days before, Dylan had married Caitlin Macnamara in Penzance Registry Office, 'with no money, no prospect of money, no attendant friends or relatives, and in complete happiness'. (The first meeting of Dylan and Caitlin is related by Augustus John in *Dylan Thomas: The Legend and the Poet*, pp. 25–28.)

The next six letters were all written from Mrs Macnamara's house at Ringford, Hants, where Dylan and his wife were staying. 'This is a very lovely place. Caitlin and I ride into the New Forest every day.' Dylan asks Watkins to type a couple of copies of a poem for him and to let him have them as quickly

---

* At one time, however, Thomas appears to have joined the Communist party.

as possible 'because I need, terribly urgently, the little money it will get me'. In November 1937, Dylan refers to a reading which he is to give at London University, at which he intends to read some of his own poems, others by Watkins, Auden, Ransom, Yeats and Prokosch. In a letter written in the following year (February 1938), Dylan refers to this University reading. 'I didn't like the people at all; some looked like lemons, and all spoke with the voices of puddings. I detest the humility I should have, and am angry when I am humble.' He refers in this letter to the fact that rhymes are coming to him naturally, which he distrusts: 'I like looking for connections, not finding them tabulated in stations.' A letter in March 1938 contains an apology for not writing for such a time because the poet has been 'in London, in penury, and in doubt: In London because money lives and breeds there; in penury, because it doesn't; and in doubt as to whether I should continue as an outlaw or take my fate for a walk in the straight and bowler-treed paths. The conceit of outlaws is a wonderful thing; they think they can join the ranks of regularly-conducted society whenever they like' (*Letters*, p. 37). This is an important statement: Dylan was then twenty-four and had little or no money; he had no particular training for any job and no experience apart from his brief period on the Swansea weekly newspaper. It is at least possible that Caitlin was beginning to demand a little more security in her life. This letter contains a good example of Dylan Thomas's kind of literary criticism. Discussing three poems which Watkins had sent him he writes,

All the words are lovely, but they *seem* so *chosen*, not struck out. I can see the sensitive picking of words, but none of the strong, inevitable pulling that makes a poem an event, a happening, an action perhaps, not a still-life or an experience put down, placed down, regulated. ... I think I ask you for a little creative destruction, destructive creation (*Letters*, p. 38).

He refers in this letter to a series of simple, straightforward stories about Swansea, one of which had been finished and published.

By July 1938, Dylan and his wife were living in Laugharne, Carmarthenshire, at first in Gosport Street and then in a house which had been recommended by Augustus John. Laugharne, says the latter, is 'one of the few "unreformed boroughs" in the kingdom, and flourishes under the mild rule of a *Port-Reeve*'. In a letter written on 5 July 1938, Dylan refers to a story *One Warm Saturday* which he has almost finished. By October 1938, Dylan is 'awfully busy' with his work, and also with reviewing, and 'muddled up with trying to get money from a sinister philanthropic society'; he says they are 'much too poor' to go and visit Watkins. Another letter written in October 1938, states that Dylan is going to Manchester to take part in a broadcast entitled *The Modern Must*. He had read a free, rhymed translation of the German Novalis's hymn 'Wenn Alle Untreue Werden', which he thought 'must be great in the original'.

Dylan and Caitlin then returned to Caitlin's mother's house, where they stayed until their baby was born. The first letter, dated 20 December 1938, refers to Dylan's recent sojourn in London: 'It is really an insane city, and filled me with terror. . . . I'm not going to London again for years; its intelligentsia is so hurried in the head that nothing stays there; its glamour smells of goat; there's no difference between good and bad.' Dylan says they are 'just as poor, or poorer'. He went up to London again in January 1939, meeting Henry Miller, Lawrence Durrell and Cameron: he says he hopes to be back in Laugharne in early spring. His son, Llewellyn, was born on 28 January 1939. In a letter written in March, Dylan refers to the imminent publication of his book *The Map of Love*. By April he and Caitlin are back in Laugharne, 'still, of course, without a penny'; the letters which he wrote to Watkins until December 1939 all come from Laugharne, where he met the author Richard Hughes, owner of Laugharne Castle. Hughes might well be the prototype of Lord Cut-Glass in *Under Milk Wood*. Dylan wrote, 'Richard Hughes lives in a castle at the top of the hill; I live in a shed at the bottom'.

Some of these letters written in 1939 are very important to the student of Dylan Thomas's poetry as giving an insight into the creative act of the poet's mind. (See especially the letter on pp. 66–8 of the *Letters*.)

In August 1939, Dylan says he is busy with 'pot-boiling stories for a book, semi-autobiographical'; he is also 'lazy – messing about in the sun and the pub'; and 'worried, by the nearness of this monstrous and still incredible war'. On 1 September he writes that 'War seems to have begun. . . . I can't kill and so, I suppose, will have to join the dangerous RAMC.' The last letter from Laugharne in 1939 came in December. As Vernon Watkins suggests in his 'Introduction' to the *Letters*, 'The point of balance in the letters is perhaps

1939, the year in which he abandoned the struggling, symbol-charged prose of the intensely subjective early stories and began to write stories about human beings living and be-having as they used to live and behave when he was a child . . . both in poetry and in prose his work from this time forward moved in the direction of the living voice'. Dylan had been happy in Laugharne: 'The peace and beauty of this small sea-town beyond Carmarthen, a fishing village at the end of the world, represented for him the last refuge of life and sanity in a nightmare world, the last irregular protest against the regular-ity and symmetry of madness. . . . The calmest and happiest days of his life were probably those he spent in Wales. The chief part of his writing was done in the landscape and among the people to whom he was most deeply attached. He was able in Laugharne to work continuously almost every afternoon. In London, where he had so many social contacts and where so many dramatic masks were expected of him, he could not work at all.'

2 His life and work 1940—53

In early 1940 Dylan and Caitlin returned to Ringwood. Although Dylan was undoubtedly happier in Laugharne than anywhere else, his wife had retrospectively some unpleasant things to say about it in *Leftover Life to Kill*. She refers to Laugharne as 'this moist, smothering, lost bog-hole, stiff with beautiful inertia, romantic nostalgias; and crass lazy people: they are sunk between worship of pennies and the decadence of initiative' (p. 15). The next passage is strangely reminiscent of *Under Milk Wood* (p. 9): 'Oh, what'll the neighbours say, what'll the neighbours . . .'. She admits that some of them were 'even lovable people', but these were 'the exceptions to the narrow, sly, keen, prodding-fingered, always counting the cost Welsh. Their most compulsive motive is fear: fear of the elements; key the door quick against the thieving night; fear of the neighbours; what will the *neigh*bours say? precisely that; fear of en*joy*ment: they roll the word round their lasci-vious tongues with condemnatory gusto' (p 15). Although Dylan Thomas refers to Llaregyb as a 'place of love', Laugharne to his wife is a 'city of lying down lying', a 'city of unheard laughter', 'deadpan Laugharne', a 'God-forsaken, Dylan-shared, vanishing dip in the hills'.

Dylan had corrected the proofs of *Portrait of the Artist as a*

Young Dog; Watkins had suggested that this title should be scrapped, but the publisher advised on its retention for 'money-making reasons'. In March 1940, Dylan refers to a visit to London 'to see about a possible, but very improbable job' that would keep him 'from pleading or soldiering. To do with films: I shan't get it'.

In August 1940, Dylan and Caitlin moved to John Davenport's house near Chippenham, and were living with a number of writers, artists and musicians, who had been offered hospitality. He informs Watkins that he wants a job very badly, because he is once again penniless, and that he has applied for a BBC job but thinks that his lack of a university education will go against him. He then collaborated with John Davenport on a detective story entitled *Death of the King's Canary*, and began to write scripts 'to be translated into, and broadcast to, Brazil'.

In a letter sent from Chippenham, probably in August 1940, he says that he has 'no visible means of support' and has 'been known to call the war bloody and silly'. He has 'begun to think about a story called *Adventures in the Skin Trade*'.

Several letters in Watkins's collection are written from Laugharne, the first being dated May 1941. Dylan was still without money. It is probably true to say that he was so long without money that when he finally began to make some he dissipated it without thought. 'This is getting ridiculous', he writes. 'The joke has gone too far. It isn't fair to be penniless *every* morning. Every morning but one, okay; but no, *every* morning.' There is another reference to the unfinished novel *Adventures in the Skin Trade*: 'My novel blathers on. It is a mixture of Oliver Twist, Little Dorrit, Kafka, Beachcomber and good old 3-adjectives-a-penny belly-churning. Thomas, the Rimbaud of Cwmdonkin Park.' The reference to Dickens is interesting because Caitlin wrote (*Leftover Life to Kill*, pp. 55–6): 'He read interminable Dickens novels, to which he was loyally devoted, and when Dylan was loyally devoted no sentimental verbosities would change him, though he did bog down somewhere in *Little Dorrit*. He categorically refused to look at Proust, Jane Austen [this is not true, according to his own letter of 25 October 1937], Tolstoy, Dostoievsky, and a lot of the obvious classics. . . .'

Dylan Thomas was found unfit for military service and hence spent most of the period of the war in Wales, visiting London to do broadcasts, meet his publishers or meet friends.

He saw much of Vernon Watkins during the period 1942–4, when the latter was on short leave passes from his unit. Watkins had met Thomas shortly after his first book, *18 Poems*, was published. It is intereting to hear that Dylan read to Watkins not only poems which were to be published later in *Twenty Five Poems* but also stories, one of the first being 'The Orchard', printed in *The Faber Book of Modern Stories*; it was in this story that the trickname Llareggub first appeared. 'Dylan alone', writes Watkins, 'could have devised so Welsh an invention, but it was also an example of the word-play he had learned from Joyce, his most admired prose-writer, whose "Dubliners" made him deprecate his own stories. "Llareggub" became, much later, the provisional title of *Under Milk Wood*, and was printed as such in the first version, half of which was published in *Botteghe Oscure* in 1951' (*Letters to Vernon Watkins*, pp. 13–14).

It was a good thing that Dylan had his refuge in Laugharne. As Caitlin tells us, 'The home was to Dylan, more especially, a private sanctum, where for once he was not compelled, by himself admittedly, to put on an act, to be amusing, to perpetuate the myth of the *Enfant Terrible*: one of the most damaging myths, and a curse to grow out of' (C. Thomas, *Leftover Life to Kill*, p. 34). Vernon Watkins has also said that Laugharne 'represented for him the last refuge of life and sanity in a nightmare world, the last irregular protest against the regularity and symmetry of madness'. His wife did all she could 'to make him work, at his own special work, and not public money-making work. And it was only with our kind of purely vegetable background, which entailed months on end of isolated, stodgy dullness and drudgery for me, that he was flattened out enough to be able to concentrate' (op. cit., p. 35).

Life in Laugharne was very simple. According to Caitlin Thomas, Dylan spent the best part of the morning in Brown's Hotel, placing bets on horses, listening to local gossip and drinking numerous pints of beer. After a late lunch he would retire to 'his humble shed, nesting high above the estuary; and bang into intensive scribbling, muttering, whispering, intoning, bellowing and juggling of words; till seven o'clock prompt' (op. cit., p. 36). In the evening he would return to Brown's or 'one of the alternative dumps'.

The war was not used by Dylan Thomas as a subject, but two of his poems, 'Deaths and Entrances' and 'A Refusal to Mourn' have the bombing raids on London as background.

The hand-to-mouth existence continued during the war years. As a result of the publication of *18 Poems* Dylan Thomas made the acquaintance of the 'bohemian side' of the London literary world at an early age, and depended greatly on his friends' generosity and hospitality. In the circumstances one can feel only respect and admiration for Caitlin Thomas's patience and self-denial. Dylan Thomas suffered in more than one way from catching the public eye a little too early. Louis MacNeice was aware of this when he wrote, 'The next few years will obviously see a spate of writing about Thomas – his vision, imagery, technique, etc. – and the writers will be beset by two distinct and opposite dangers – the danger of trying to equip him too exactly with a literary pedigree and the danger of isolating him as a wild sport, a Villon figure, a wild man who threw up works of genius without knowing what he was doing' (*Dylan Thomas: The Legend and the Poet, A Critical Symposium*, pp. 85–7).

Roy Campbell has given us a few brief details of Dylan's life in London: they both obtained 'considerable radio jobs' at the same time, but Campbell admits that he got his by chance, whilst Dylan got his 'through his own deserts, the beauty of his voice and its amazing strength . . .'. Campbell says later that 'Dylan was the best all-round reader of verse' that he had ever produced on the BBC, but he could not real correct poets like Pope or Dryden. Dylan not only read poetry for the BBC but also prose-readings from Cervantes and W. H. Davies (*Dylan Thomas: The Legend and the Poet, A Critical Symposium*, pp. 41–45). Lawrence Durrell in the same book refers to Dylan's 'curious pulpiteer's thrasonical voice' (p. 38). Louis MacNeice says that 'he had a natural sense of theatre . . . he was, moreover, a subtle and versatile actor, as he proved repeatedly in radio performances. . . . Though his special leaning (as was natural, gives his astonishing voice) was to the sonorous and emotional, he enjoyed playing character parts, especially comic or grotesque ones' (p. 86).

Dylan Thomas's semi-autobiographical short stories, *Portrait of the Artist as a Young Dog*, were published in 1941, in which the author portrayed his 'public' personality – the personality of a self-conscious entertainer. His sketches and short stories are 'brilliant improvisations, which were fundamentally an extension of his genius for conversation' (*Dylan Thomas*, p. 7).

There are not many letters to Vernon Watkins after 1941.

One is written from the business address of the magazine *Horizon*, and Dylan says that his lack of money is endurable in London, but he is still looking for a film job and has been offered several scripts to do 'in the near future'. Vernon Watkins lost all the letters which came in the next two and a half years, and the following letter is dated July 1944. Dylan says he is looking for somewhere to live in the country – 'in Laugharne, if possible'. His daughter, Aeronwy, had been born in 1943. A letter in the following month comes from Llangain, near Carmarthen. A second letter in the same month says that Dylan and his family are moving into a new house in New Quay, Cardiganshire. A letter written in October 1944 refers to a film company 'who pay me occasionally', and one has the impression that Dylan was better off than he ever had been.

For a short time he and his family lived at Oxford: in a letter written from here Dylan admits that he has not worked for a long time 'apart from reading, every week, over the air to Indians'. The Oxford period was followed by a holiday in Ireland – in Dublin and Kerry, which Dylan apparently enjoyed very much. By March 1947, he is intimating that they will be going to Italy (a brief note on this visit by Mario Luzi is in *Dylan Thomas: The Legend and the Poet*, pp. 48–9). In the summer he left Florence for Elba and wrote the poem 'In Country Sleep'.

Details of Dylan Thomas's tours in the USA are given in J. M. Brinnin's *Dylan Thomas in America*, which also has interesting sections on Laugharne and London. The poetry-reading tours were undertaken to make money. Brinnin's book, as Fraser says, is 'almost agonizingly accurate in its description of many embarrassing episodes, but it is a portrait of a sick man under the strain of financial and moral worry, and of being perpetually on public show, and it should not be taken as giving a fair idea of the character or the personality of Dylan Thomas as his English friends knew him' (*Dylan Thomas*, p. 9).

Brinnin's book is of interest to the student of *Under Milk Wood* in that it shows the last stages of development of the play. In 1952 (p. 151) he said that *Llareggub Hill* (its title at that time) 'was coming on well enough and that he hoped to have a final draft within two or three months'. When Brinnin suggested that the play might furnish him with a completely new programme for his American tour, 'he was dubious about thinking in terms of a production, even a minimal reading production, mainly because *authentic Welsh accents would be essential*' (editor's italics). He agreed to have a completed script ready by March 1953. It was Brinnin who suggested that the title *Llareggub Hill* be changed. 'The joke in the present title was a small and childish one, he felt; beyond that, the word "Llareggub" would be too thick and forbidding to attract American audiences. "What about Under Milk Wood?", he said, and I said "Fine", and the new work was christened on the spot.'

Dylan arrived for the last time in New York on 21 April 1953, and *Under Milk Wood* was still far from finished. It was arranged that Dylan should read the still unfinished play in a solo performance on 3 May. 'As a solo piece, *Under Milk Wood* afforded him every opportunity to demonstrate his skill as a reader and, to the surprise of a great part of his audience, his ingenuity as an actor. He was constantly interrupted by extended bursts of laughter, and the play proceeded in an atmosphere of crackling excitement from its first solemn moments to its later passages of zany comedy and its final mellow embrace of a whole village of the living and the dead' (Brinnin, op. cit., pp. 167–8).

By September 1953, the script of *Under Milk Wood* was fairly complete and, under his direction, 'the new version . . . fairly leaped into shape'. New scenes of the play were, however, still being dictated by the author, who now began to be very ill. He complained that he had 'felt as sick as death all the way over' from London. A doctor who, months before, had warned him that 'only a rigorous and unbroken regime would begin to relieve him of his physical torment' was called in. Soon after this *Under Milk Wood* was given its third reading, with final additions incorporated into the script. On Sunday, 25 October, a matinee of *Under Milk Wood* was held; it was the last in which he was to participate, and by every report its greatest performance. 'A thousand people were left hushed by its lyrical harmonies and its grandeur, among them Robert Shaw, the eminent choral director, who came backstage and, moved to tears, expressed his admiration' (Brinnin, *Dylan Thomas in America*, p. 215).

The death of Dylan Thomas has been described by J. M. Brinnin. Dylan Thomas's body was brought back from New York to Laugharne, where he was buried in November 1953. During these last years he had lived in Oxfordshire and again in Laugharne; he had made four trips to the USA and a trip to Persia to write a documentary film about oil. He had been a sick man for some time as a result not only of his mode of living but also of the financial and moral worry which beset him. The village publican attended the funeral and, as he walked away, exclaimed, 'He was a very *humble* man'. In the period that followed there was a great show of public mourning and legend-building unequalled, so far as literary figures are concerned, in modern times. Dame Edith Sitwell sent the following telegram to Laugharne, 'To the greatest poet of the younger generation lying in his grave I send devotion undying as his poetry is deathless'.

For further details the student should consult:

Dylan Thomas: The Legend and the Poet, A Critical Symposium, edited by E. W. Tedlock.
Dylan Thomas: Letters to Vernon Watkins, edited with an introduction by Vernon Watkins.
G. S. Fraser *Dylan Thomas.*
J. M. Brinnin *Dylan Thomas in America.*
Caitlin Thomas *Leftover Life to Kill.*
Dylan Thomas *Portrait of the Artist as a Young Dog.*

3 The poetry of Dylan Thomas

A list of Dylan Thomas's publications will be found on page 91. It is suggested that the student of *Under Milk Wood* should at least read some of the poems in *Collected Poems* and some of the short stories.

It should be stressed at the outset that Dylan Thomas was a true Welshman (never a 'professional' Welshman) in the natural qualities of his poetry — 'its high emotional charge and sonorous rhetoric, and the lilt and exaggeration of its phrasing'. Much of his subject-matter (stories, later poems, *Under Milk Wood*) was also derived from Wales. His technique also shows affinities with Welsh poets past and present, and it would be ludicrous to suggest that he was not aware of some of the principles of Welsh prosody. English does not lend itself readily to the complex metrical tricks and patterns of Welsh, but Dylan Thomas's techniques are of the same general type as the Welsh. His particular interest in consonantal chime, or *cynghanedd*, might have been stimulated by Hopkins's use of it, but, as Geoffrey Moore pointed out, 'Thomas is more tricky than Hopkins. Where Hopkins uses rhyme and alliteration for the sake of more music, Thomas will, when he feels like it, amuse himself with verse-patterns which add nothing to the music of the verse at all and, in fact, have only a curiosity value' (another essay titled 'Dylan Thomas', by Shapiro, is cited on p. 28, in *Dylan Thomas: The Legend and the Poet, A Critical Symposium*, pp. 248–68).

Henry Treece has pointed out (*Dylan Thomas*, 'Dog Among the Fairies', p. 10) the dualism in Dylan Thomas's make-up. On the one hand he was an introverted romantic poet, but as a man he was an extrovert. It is doubtful whether he could have become either novelist or playwright, since he lacked patience and staying-power to become a novelist, and his stories are those of a lyric poet. His play *Under Milk Wood* similarly provides no evidence that he could have become a conventional playwright, for it is 'a series of labyrinthine, microscopic insights, magnificently moving in its separate unit, but blurred and static when seen as a whole. Nothing seems to *happen* (which makes it so true a picture of a small town, of course) apart from the varied beating of the hearts in a hundred rooms. It bears no more relation to a play than does a clock-maker's shop, where the many machines tick out their day at speeds and tones dictated by their individual mechanisms. Or, to use another metaphor, *Under Milk Wood* is an anthill, which is quite static from a distance of ten yards, and only comes to life when observed from ten inches.' 'It is a pointilliste technique too refined for the theatre' (Treece, op. cit., p. 13). Dylan Thomas himself said that his poetry was a collection of images, related or unrelated, as they occurred to him. 'Each image holds within it the seed of its own destruction, and my dialectal [i.e. dialectical] method ... is a constant building up and breaking down of the images that come out of the central seed, which is itself destructive and constructive at the same time.' Some part of the obscurity is undoubtedly to be attributed to the very long period of gestation of each poem, and the frequent alterations which were made on the basis of whether the poet himself found the result satisfying, no matter what its 'meaning' might have been. His wife refers to him as 'a punctilious, pettifogging niggler for detail'. For him poetry was an act of *making*: there were no 'rules' in poetry – 'You made your own rules and it either was or wasn't a poem' (Caitlin Thomas, *Leftover Life to Kill*, p. 68). Caitlin also suggests that there are many lines in

Dylan's poetry of which he had long ago forgotten the 'meaning'. One suspects that the following statement, substituting *poem* for speech, could well have been made by Dylan: 'The essence of a good speech is not sense, but the conviction behind it, and the flow of words; hesitation is fatal; also the volume is important' (*Leftover Life to Kill*, p. 180).

Though Dylan Thomas's early poems showed obvious influences, such as those of Hopkins, Swinburne, Joyce and Yeats, their impact on the poetry-reading public was something new and fresh. It is a matter for the individual student to decide whether he agrees or not with Holbrook that much of Thomas's poetry is meaningless or whether he allows Tindall (*A Reader's Guide to Dylan Thomas*) to find 'meanings' which the poet did not intend. 'What seems to be complexity is often mere irresponsibility or laziness in leaving a half-finished figure – often it is a deliberate perversity' (Holbrook, *Llareggub Revisited*, p. 121). The first perversity, says Holbrook, is irresponsibility about *punctuation*, which 'produces perplexity' in the reader, and is intended to stand instead of 'genuine complexity and involvement', and is thus an affectation. Another type of irresponsibility is syntactical, verbal irresponsibility. 'Everything is left to chance and sound – in the Sitwellian way – and language is handled for effect from the outside, not from the deep inward intractable voice of true metaphor.' Another type of syntactical irresponsibility is the *deliberate manipulation of the syntax* to increase ambiguity, 'so that it becomes meaningless in the ordinary meaning of the word'. Holbrook admits that he finds forty-two of the ninety poems in Dylan Thomas's *Collected Poems* 'meaningless, or yielding no meaning worth possessing even with the most considerable effort'. Of fifteen poems, he 'can make nothing at all' (*Llareggub Revisited*, p. 127).

This is not, primarily, a book on the poems of Dylan Thomas. The reader must taste them for himself and, if interested, have a look at the highly critical attitudes of David Holbrook. The present writer can only confess that he is affected by some of them, in spite of Holbrook's ferocious strictures. The intellectual argument of a poem is often replaced in Thomas's poems by a highly conscious attention to texture which he shares with Gerard Manley Hopkins and Edith Sitwell. The sound is often more important than the literal sense, which may indeed be totally absent; it is often the sound which provides a poem's dynamic, and one has the impression that Dylan Thomas heard them aloud long before he began to give *hwyl*-inspired readings. Thomas's poetry expresses 'the contradictions between glory and decay, between entrance into the world and death, between flesh and ghost. It is in its final phases a religious poetry' (J. M. Cohen, *Poetry of This Age*). He was a naturally unintellectual poet, and the connecting thread of many of his poems is a dream-like association from his childhood memories. He himself was aware of this:

> When Logics die
> The secret of the soil grows through the eye,
>   And blood jumps in the sun (*18 Poems*).

18 Poems (published 1934). All of these poems appear in their original order in *Collected Poems* and were written in 1933 and 1934 during Thomas's 'womb-tomb period'. Their themes are creation (physical and poetic) and the temporal process of birth, death and re-birth. Some of the poems have a socialistic tinge, some are dreamlike. The note of fear is predominant: fear of impending war, sexual experience and literary failure. One can agree with Tindall that some of his best poems are to be found in these early ones. They deal largely with 'something humanly undignified, adolescent frustration' and bestow upon it 'natural dignity' (Fraser). The reader approaching them for the first time will find fascinating attempts at elucidation of some of the more obscure points in Tindall's *A Reader's Guide to Dylan Thomas* (pp. 38–87). One must often admire Tindall's analytical ingenuity, but sometimes he overdoes it a little, as he himself is aware. 'The danger of guessing the senses of a thing like this is that idea, replacing poem, will drive out marvel.'

The first poem in *18 Poems* shows two of Thomas's favourite devices: *dissonance* – an approximate rhyme in which vowels disagree and consonants agree (e.g. *goat-gate*), a form of *cynghanedd*; and *assonance* – an approximate rhyme in which consonants disagree and vowels agree (e.g. *rake-pain*). The second poem 'Where Once the Twilight Locks no Longer', has creation for its theme, and uses dissonance in the manner of Yeats, Owen and Auden. The fourth poem is the one which established Thomas's fame – 'The Force that through the Green Fuse Drives the Flower'. Tindall asks, 'What other poet of that time, Yeats aside, could compose a thing so simple and so rich, so dense and so clear?' Its imagery, rhythm and

sound-pattern show unmistakably the influences of Gerard
Manley Hopkins. The poem 'Where once the Waters of Your
Face' is one of Thomas's finest lyrics, elaborating a single
metaphor: the womb is the sea, which also figures prominently
in *Under Milk Wood*. Thomas's trick of reversal is found here –
'lovebeds of the weeds' is probably weedbeds of the loves (cf.
'pig-loving sun' in *Under Milk Wood*).

The four sonnets of 'Our Eunuch Dreams' are formally
based on Hopkins's 'Pied Beauty'. In the poem 'When, Like a
Running Grave' we have an illustration of Freud's influence in
'the kissproof world', 'kissproof' includes both desire and
frustration; as a type of lipstick it includes Freudian 'lip' and
'stick', 'death's agents and lovers' delights. Joyce had a hand
in such doubling talk' (Tindall, op. cit., p. 67). (It should be
noted that Thomas hinted in a letter to Vernon Watkins that
obscurity was a protective device. 'Is obscurity', asks Tindall,
'a disguise for commonplace matter or an activity of the
Freudian censor?' (Tindall, op. cit., p. 112).)

The poem 'In the Beginning' shows Thomas's preoccupation with the Old Testament – 'Genesis was the book for
Thomas, in love with creation, whether of world, child or
poem, the three analogous creatures of the Word' (Tindall,
op. cit., p. 69).

'Light Breaks Where no Sun Shines' shows technical features
also found in *Under Milk Wood* – assonance (shines, tides,
light), interwoven with an *s*-consonance. The theme of 'I
Fellowed Sleep' seems to be Freudian – that of the 'Oedipus
Complex'.

The above brief notes serve only to indicate some of the
influences which can already be discerned in Thomas's work,
particularly the Bible, Yeats, Freud and James Joyce. (For an
unflattering comparison with Joyce, see Holbrook's strictures
on certain passages in *Under Milk Wood*, in *Llareggub Revisited*, pp. 213–18.) In these early poems Thomas was
attempting to find symbols for his adolescent experience; some
of the symbolism was to appear again twenty years later in
Under Milk Wood.

Twenty Five Poems (published in 1936). The slim volume *18
Poems* went largely unnoticed by the general reading public,
but considerable praise was lavished on his second book of
poems and, after Edith Sitwell's review of it in *The Observer*,
Thomas acquired a reputation as a poet. Some of the poems

were written in 1935 and 1936, but the volume also contains poems resuscitated from his 1930–33 notebooks. There are new themes and images, and some poems show the influence both of Yeats and of Rainer Maria Rilke, whom Thomas had read in translation (a letter to Vernon Watkins shows that he knew no German). The most important poems in this book are the ten sonnets beginning 'Altar-wise by Candlelight' (analysed by Tindall in *A Reader's Guide to Dylan Thomas*, pp. 137–54). The sonnets are important because 'they announce the current of orthodox Christian feeling – feeling rather than thought – which was henceforth increasingly to dominate Thomas's work in poetry' (Fraser). *The Map of Love* (published 1939) contains sixteen poems as well as stories; these poems re-appear in the *Collected Poems* and were written between 1937 and 1939 (a few between 1930 and 1933). Some of these poems are reminiscent of certain passages in *Under Milk Wood*, e.g. 'Once it was the Colour of Saying' (*Collected Poems*, p. 89),

> Pale rain over the dwindling harbour
> Over the sea-wet church the size of a snail . . .

In 'A Saint About to Fall' (*Collected Poems*, pp. 95–6) the poet writes,

> O wake me in my house in the mud
> of the crotch of the squawking shores . . .

which refers to Dylan Thomas's house at Laugharne in which he has sought refuge from the 'carbolic city' of London.

Deaths and Entrances (published in 1946) was Dylan Thomas's last English volume of new poems – there was a limited edition of *Twenty-Six Poems*, published in 1950 in Verona, Italy, and the small volume of six poems, *In Country Sleep*, published in 1952 at Norfolk, Connecticut. Most of the poems of *Deaths and Entrances* were written during the war years. *In Country Sleep* originally contained the poem 'Do Not Go Gentle', which is in the *Deaths and Entrances* section of *Collected Poems*. One poem is of particular interest to the student of *Under Milk Wood*, 'When I Woke',

> When I woke, the town spoke.
> Birds and clocks and cross bells
> Dinned aside the coiling crowd . . .

As Tindall has said, the first line could serve as an epitaph for *Under Milk Wood*.

4 Some 'influences' on Dylan Thomas

Dylan Thomas has been described (Christine Brooke-Rose, *A Grammar of Metaphor*, London, 1958, p. 323) as 'the strange but logical conclusion of Shakespeare, Keats and Hopkins on the one hand, Blake, Yeats and Eliot on the other – the fusion of grammatical metaphor and symbolism'. The author quoted finds Dylan Thomas 'the most highly metaphoric' of all the fifteen poets she selected for analysis in this fascinating book. Thomas has the highest percentage in 'Simple Replacement' metaphors and a high percentage in 'Genitive Links'. 'Many of them are in prolonged metaphor, like a brief allegory, but his allegories often leave reality altogether to assume their own weird logic, so that the metaphors can seem quasi-literal.' She finds a lack of architecture in Thomas's poems: the poet relies on the interaction of words and the poems are static, their ends saying exactly the same as the beginnings, 'but in different metaphoric terms, however well integrated, like a fugue and variations, with the theme perhaps turned upside down. Hence the rhetorical repetitions of the same syntactic formulae with different words. His metaphors are the orchestration of the same theme, each one striking a chord in the mind with previous metaphors. The poem, in fact, has to be static: if a new concept were introduced the metaphoric language, with its chain reaction of development and contradiction, would probably collapse.' Particularly noticeable is Thomas's use of *adjective metaphors*;* there is also in his work considerable development of *adverb metaphors** and *preposition metaphors*.*

It is not proposed here to attempt any exhaustive evaluation of all the possible influences and sources of Dylan Thomas's poetry, but a few words will be useful on the modern influences, including those of Freud.

Thomas Hardy (1840–1928) novelist and poet, was born in Dorset and articled to an architect, but advised to write by George Meredith. His first popular success was with his novel *Far From the Madding Crowd* (1874). From 1909 until his death he wrote only lyric poetry. It is generally recognized that Hardy's genius is more represented by his poetry than his novels.

* For an explanation of these terms see the book quoted.

See Hardy, *Collected Poems*; or *Selected Poems* (ed. G. M. Young); Sir Maurice Bowra, *The Lyrical Poetry of Hardy*. (Hardy was Dylan Thomas's favourite poet of the century, and Yeats he considered as the greatest living poet.)

Gerard Manley Hopkins (1844–89) was born in London and educated at Highgate School and Balliol College, Oxford. In 1866 he was converted to the Roman Catholic faith and in 1868 entered the Jesuit novitiate; he was ordained priest in 1877. During his lifetime his work was not published and even after his death only a few poems appeared until Robert Bridges edited the poems in 1918 (revised edition, London, 1930; enlarged edition, edited W. H. Gardner, London, 1948).

The language of Dylan Thomas is close to that of Hopkins, not only in obvious ways but also in its very method (see K. Shapiro's essay 'Dylan Thomas' in *Dylan Thomas: The Legend and the Poet, A Critical Symposium*, pp. 269–83). The main difference between Hopkins and Thomas, suggests Shapiro, is that the former drew his symbology from the God-symbol, the latter almost entirely from the Sex-symbol.

Hopkins was himself a technical innovator, eschewing stock rhythms and worn-out vocabulary. He concentrated on the distinctive individuality of things, which he termed the *inscape*. He called his principle of rhythm *sprung rhythm*, which rests upon the attitude that English is a language of *stress*, and that, therefore, English verse cannot be strictly quantitative. In Hopkins there is frequent *alliteration*.

See Hopkins, *Poems* (ed. W. H. Gardner); W. H. Gardner, *Gerard Manley Hopkins*, 2 vols.

William Butler Yeats (1865–1939) was an Irish poet and leading member of the 'Celtic Revival'. He contributed to the *Yellow Book* and published his poems *Wanderings of Oisin* in 1889. In 1897 he helped to found what became the Abbey Theatre, Dublin, for which he composed several plays, e.g. *The Countess Cathleen* (1892), *The Pot of Broth* (1902), *On Baile's Strand* (1904). His critical works include *Ideas of Good and Evil* (1903) and *Plays and Controversies* (1923). His fame rests upon his lyrics, of which he published many volumes: *The Wind Among the Reeds* (1899), *The Wild Swans at Coole* (1919), *The Tower* (1928), and *The Winding Stair* (1933). His poetry is essentially Irish in inspiration and character. Yeats became a Senator of the Irish Free State (1922–8) and was awarded the Nobel Prize for Literature in 1923.

See Yeats, *Collected Poems*; L. MacNeice, *The Poetry of W. B. Yeats;* P. Ure, *Towards a Mythology: Studies in the Poetry of Yeats*.

James Joyce (1882–1941) novelist and poet, was born in Dublin and studied there and in Paris. His first volume of poetry was *Chamber Music* (1907). His collection of short stories, *Dubliners*, appeared in 1914, and his *Portrait of the Artist as a Young Man* in 1916. He acquired international fame with the publication of *Ulysses* (Paris, 1922; England, 1936). From 1922 to 1939 he worked on *Finnegan's Wake*, which was published in parts.

Undoubtedly Joyce exercised a powerful influence on Dylan Thomas. The file in which the latter kept his poems was significantly entitled *Pomes*, and his semi-autobiographical short stories were influenced by *Dubliners*. It is also interesting to note that *Ulysses* begins with a detailed moving evocation of the awakening hours of a city and its people (compare *Under Milk Wood*).

See T. S. Eliot, *Introducing Joyce: a Selection of Prose*; H. Kenner, *Dublin's Joyce*.

A Note on Cynghanedd: Cynghanedd may be described as a Welsh alliterative device or a device consisting partly of internal rhyme and alliteration.

The word *cynghanedd* literally means 'harmony' and is a method of giving pattern to a line by the echoing of both consonantal and vowel sounds. There are three main divisions of *cynghanedd*:

  i) *cynghanedd gytsain*: multiple alliteration;
 ii) *cynghanedd sain*: alliteration and rhyme within the line;
iii) *cynghanedd lusg*: internal rhyme only. The second variety was much used in English by Gerard Manley Hopkins. An example of it, given by Gwyn Williams, is,

The road with its load of lads.

An example of the third variety is,

A saint in an old painting.

The *rhyming-assonance* patterns found in Dylan Thomas's poetry are not strictly *cynghanedd*, 'but in keeping with the idea of it. It is a more meticulous and, in a way, a more wilful patterning than Hopkins allowed himself, and to this extent more Welsh. . . . In so far as Thomas's verse is in keeping with an attitude to poetry which involved complicated patterns it may be called Welsh in feeling' (Geoffrey Moore, 'Dylan Thomas' in *Dylan Thomas: The Legend and the Poet, A Critical Symposium*, pp. 254–7).

The student should consider the following lines from Shakespeare (*pr - f - l*),

> Was it the proud full sail of his great verse
> Bound for the prize of all-too-precious you. . . .

and (*t - d - s, t - d - s*)

> O, he's tedious
> As a tired horse. . . .
> (*Henry IV*, Part 1.)

On *cynghanedd* see Glyn Williams, *An Introduction to Welsh Poetry*, Appendix A; Thomas Parry, *A History of Welsh Literature*, Appendix to Chapter V.

Freud (1856–1939) Sigmund Freud was born in 1856; he was a Jewish psychologist and founder of psycho-analysis.

Psycho-analysis is a term used to denote three different things – firstly, a special method of medical treatment used for the cure of certain nervous disorders; secondly, a special technique for investigating the 'deeper layers' of the mind; thirdly, that branch of knowledge which has developed as a result of the exercise of the special technique, and which is generally described as 'the science of the unconscious'.

It had long been suspected that the mind contains elements not accessible to consciousness (see L. L. Whyte, *The Unconscious before Freud*). According to Whyte, it was only after the time of Descartes that the term *unconscious mind* really became a part of European thought. According to Freud, the mind can be compared to a series of 'compartments', communication between which is actively prevented by the operation of definite factors.

Freud based his techniques on the theory that mental disorders and certain abnormalities of behaviour result from *conflicts* between the unconscious mind and *repressed* ideas.

'Depth psychology' recognizes that mental forces are stratified or 'compartmentalized' and that there is an incessant interplay of inner forces in an effort to arrive at a compromise among themselves to the life of the 'external world'. According to the depth psychologists, there are two groups of instincts: the 'ego-instincts' and the 'object-instincts'. The Freudian school regards the ego-instincts as the reservoir of sexual urges, images and ideas, the impulses of self-preservation and the desire for union. These instincts manifest themselves in what is termed in psycho-analysis *libido*.

The single idea of Freud which is most generally understood is that any understanding of our present behaviour must take into account all our *previous* experiences, including those which always were or have become *unconscious*: our awareness of the significance of what we do is limited by the active residues of earlier experiences.

The Freudian theme on which the main opposition to psycho-analysis has been directed is sexuality. There is a heavy social ban on various aspects of sexuality, and ideas of morality are concentrated against the 'radiations from this central sin': the extent to which they *are* so concentrated, according to Freud, was only an echo of the internal repression of sexual impulses. The greater part of this internal repression is, however, unconscious, a pointer to the strength and depth of these impulses. Hence the part played by sexual impulses in the unconscious is much more extensive than that they play in the consciousness.

Freud's work on *dreams* is the first link he brought about between psycho-analysis and general psychology. As a result of Freud's work it has become recognized that the study of dreams is an important aspect of psychology, and that it is of very great practical value in the treatment of nervous disorders, when it is necessary to penetrate the 'deeper layers' of the mind. Freud distinguished between the *manifest* content of the dream (i.e. the dream as recorded) and the *latent* content, or the thoughts leading up to the dream; the latter are ascertained by analysing its details by the method of 'free association'. Freud held that a *wish-fulfilment* is essential to any dream, i.e. the imaginary gratification of a repressed wish.

Some of the most important applications of psychoanalysis have been in the fields of medicine, education, anthropology, sociology and politics, art and literature, criminology and law, mythology and folklore, and religion.

As regards literature, it is obvious that the formal elements of poetry, such as metre, vocabulary and rhythm, do not constitute the whole of poetry. There must also be *ideas*. Yet these ideas are the representatives of *unconscious* ideas which are accessible to psycho-analysis.

The psycho-analysis of *myths* has shown that they represent in a camouflaged manner the most primitive wishes and fears of mankind. Both the mechanism of and the motive for the disguise are similar to those of dreams.

The interest of psycho-analysis in religion lies in the fact that religious feelings and beliefs fulfil the deepest cravings of the mind and, at the same time, give some appeasement to the unconscious moral tension.

There is obviously no possibility in a short book of this nature to go into Freud's work in any detail, but it does not detract from his greatness to say much of what he put forward is still disputed, and that psycho-analysts have themselves corrected or modified some of his formulations. It must be remembered that, until Freud pointed the way, psychologists had scarcely concerned themselves with the *irrational* in human behaviour and thought.

Henry Treece has referred to Dylan Thomas's 'Freudian concept of poetry' which 'led him to the image direct' (*Dylan Thomas*, p. 46). Treece thinks that Thomas's poetry 'shows him as the Freudian "sick man" whose world is only made complete by his art. Those of his readers who are "sick" in the same way, will find in Thomas a relief from their own malady, a reintegration of the personality in a world created in their own image. For them, Dylan Thomas will be a prophet; and, what is more, a prophet on a level unexplored by those poets whose craftsman-repressions have led them to sift and refine their original poetic impulses to that stage when they can be comprehended by the greatest number of readers.'

The play

5 Introduction

The present writer has been a reader of all Dylan Thomas's works, and the point of view adopted in these *Notes* is that not only is *Under Milk Wood* the last of his works, but also, in many ways, it is the culmination of them. Whatever one's final attitude to *Under Milk Wood* may be, it is impossible fully to appreciate this play without some knowledge of Dylan Thomas's poetry and other prose-works.

From the evidence provided in Brinnin's *Dylan Thomas in America* the play was not written in its present printed sequence: the first 'portion' to be completed was Captain Cat's speech. The final version was put together under conditions of strain and pressure, but it is obvious that there had been a long period of gestation, pointers to which are found in Dylan Thomas's previous work and will be indicated in these *Notes*.

Hitherto there has been very little diagnostic or critical discussion of *Under Milk Wood*; on the other hand there are numerous studies of Dylan Thomas's poetry. The only considerable discussion of the play is that of David Holbrook in his *Llareggub Revisited*. The present writer has found Holbrook's essay both stimulating and suggestive, but does not subscribe to all his views. Very interesting indeed are Holbrook's comparisons of Dylan Thomas with James Joyce and the indication of the sources of one or two passages in *Under Milk Wood*. The student is strongly recommended to read Holbrook's essay, but not before he has read, and preferably heard (on records), the play two or three times.

It is also recommended that the student should at least 'dip into' some of the previous works of Dylan Thomas, such as his *Collected Poems*, and the prose-pieces of *Portrait of the Artist as a Young Dog*, *A Prospect of the Sea* and *Adventures in the Skin Trade*, in order to come to grips with his idiom and attitudes. The poet himself recorded some of his poems and the student should endeavour to obtain these recordings.

Some indication of the character and personality of Dylan Thomas is afforded by the *Letters to Vernon Watkins* and Brinnin's *Dylan Thomas in America*. The latter, however, in spite of its seeming genuineness and objectivity, must be treated with caution, since it deals with restricted and 'artificial' periods of the poet's life, when he was living and working under great stress.

It is necessary also to exercise caution when talking about literary 'influences'. Often a writer himself will be no more than dimly conscious of the writers who have influenced him. In the case of Dylan Thomas the first, lasting and all-pervading influence was the Bible; among writers it seems safe to say that Gerard Manley Hopkins, with his subtle linguistic experimentation, was a seminal influence. It should be remembered in this connection that Hopkins himself spent a period of his life in North Wales (St Asaph) and was, in turn, influenced by Welsh prosodical techniques, especially that of *cynghanedd*. Although Dylan Thomas did not speak Welsh, it is ludicrous to suppose that he was unaware of the complex technical devices used by Welsh bards.

James Joyce was undoubtedly another important influence, and once again it is suggested that the student should 'dip into' Joyce's work, especially *Ulysses, Portrait of the Artist as a Young Man*, the short stories *Dubliners*, and the early poems *Chamber Music*. (This could well be holiday reading for *pleasure*, rather than for examination purposes.)

Another important influence was Sigmund Freud, as revealed in the imagery and attitudes of Dylan Thomas. From the evidence available it does not seem that Dylan Thomas was a great reader, or in any way a scholarly person, but it was during his main formative period in the 1930s that popularizations of Freud's work first began to appear, such as Ernest Jones's tiny volume on *Psycho-analysis* (Benn's Sixpenny Library), or J. C. Flugel's article on the subject in *An Outline of Modern Knowledge*, published by Victor Gollancz in 1930, or G. Coster's *Psycho-analysis for Normal People*, and it is not unlikely that Dylan Thomas read one of these, or heard discussions of psycho-analytical ideas, or even read a translation of one of Freud's works, such as *The Psychopathology of Everyday Life* (published as a 'Pelican') or *The Interpretation of Dreams*. Also available in the 1930s was a translation of the Viennese doctor Groddeck's *The Book of the Id*.

Of Dylan Thomas's contemporaries perhaps the greatest influence was exercised by T. S. Eliot, and Holbrook provides an example from *Under Milk Wood* of a direct borrowing. Dylan Thomas regarded W. B. Yeats as the greatest modern

poet, and the selections he chose from Yeats, Hardy, Swinburne, Hart Crane and others for his American recitals are,
perhaps, indicative of his favourite poets. It is probable that
Dylan Thomas could, if with difficulty, read French, and
among other 'influences' may be listed those of Mallarme,
Baudelaire, Verlaine and Rimbaud. He may have read some
of these poets in translation, as was certainly the case with
Rainer Maria Rilke (translated by J. B. Leishmann), since
Dylan Thomas knew no German.

The student of *Under Milk Wood*, then, if he is to do justice
to the play and to its author, has a wide and complex field of
study. This 'play for voices' leads back to Dylan Thomas's
own previous work in both poetry and prose; to the Bible; to
other contemporary writers (including, for this purpose,
Gerard Manley Hopkins's as a 'contemporary', since Bridges
did not publish the latter's work until 1918); to Freud; to the
technical devices of Welsh poetry; and, not least, to the social
atmosphere of Dylan Thomas's own upbringing. The present
volume of *Notes* will assist the student in his early reading of
the play, and will suggest avenues of further study. Topics for
general essays and questions will be found at the end of this
book. It should be remembered that *Under Milk Wood* is
described as 'a play for voices', but on an earlier occasion
Dylan Thomas referred to it as a 'dramatic poem'. Even if one
agrees with David Holbrook that it is not 'dramatic' at all, one
must nevertheless agree that it is a *poem*. As a poem it gains
immeasurably from being spoken and, once again, it is recommended that the student should listen to the recording at the
earliest opportunity.

Note: It is not known whether Dylan Thomas read Hugh de
Selincourt's classic novel, *The Cricket Match* (first published
1924), but in some way the structure of *Under Milk Wood* is
reminiscent of it. Thus, Chapter I of *The Cricket Match* is
entitled 'Introduces the Village of Tillingford'. The commentator (corresponding to First Voice) is the author, who directs
our attention to features of the village.

Look down on the still village as the morning sun, peering over the
hills, sends rays to penetrate the gentle encircling haze. . . . From the
cottage rises the smoke of the earliest kindled fires. . . . The village is
awakening to the day.

Chapter II is entitled 'Some Players Awaken', and Chapter
III, 'The Morning Passes'. The last chapter of the book is

entitled 'The Evening Passes and Night Falls'. There is thus an essential parallelism between the structure of *Under Milk Wood* and that of *The Cricket Match*.

6 Method of study

It would be highly inadvisable for anyone to study the play without some prior reading of Dylan Thomas's poetry, obscure as much of that may be, if the attempt is made to understand it only with the intellect. It is the editor's view that Dylan Thomas was fascinated by the mere shape, sound and evocative power of words quite apart from their formal uses of semantic content, and any reader who does not respond in the same way will miss much of the lyrical beauty of the work. For *work* it was: as a craftsman Thomas was extraordinarily painstaking, and people who saw him at work refer to sheaves of notes relating to a single poem, each piece of paper containing only one line and its numerous variants. Once a poem had been written out in full, and later an alteration – perhaps of only one word or even of punctuation – was made, the whole poem would again be laboriously recopied: the detailed effects had to blend into a satisfying total effect.* This painstaking craftsmanship in the hard, recalcitrant medium of language is brought out in his *Letters to Vernon Watkins*.

Whatever one's ultimate evaluation of Dylan Thomas as a poet, there can be no doubt of his masterly craftsmanship; even so, as G. S. Fraser has remarked 'the craft exists only for the art'. Fraser suggests that Dylan Thomas's stature is possibly that of 'a major minor poet', but adds that 'we should be profoundly suspicious of this class-room, or examination-room, attitude to poets'. It has been said that if one grapples enough *some* meaning can always be elicited from even the very obscure poems (see W. Y. Tindall, *A Reader's Guide to Dylan Thomas*) but it is highly probable that Dylan Thomas was not over-concerned with the 'meaning' or 'sense' so long as the total sound-impact satisfied him. I think that G. I. Fraser has successfully shown that, at least in Thomas's best poems, there is always a 'coherent meaning' and that it is 'not always mechanically the same meaning'. Fraser wrote (*Dylan*

---

* It is possible that Dylan Thomas had heard that this was Yeats's method of composition; even for a poem such as 'Coole Park, 1929' there were 38 pages of drafts. For Yeats's method of working see *Between the Lines*, by J. Stallworthy.

Thomas, p. 33), 'It is simply not true that he went on writing, with variations of form and imagery, the same archetypal poem over and over again; he grew and changed and at his death was still developing, in the direction of a wider and more genial human scope. The importance of *Under Milk Wood* is that it shows him, at the very end of his life, transforming into a kind of poetry that humorous apprehension of life which, in *Portrait of the Artist as a Young Dog*, is still something quite separate from poetry. . . . His feeling for life was, at the end, growing not shrinking; and the separated elements of it, the outer and inner being, the legendary sweet funny man and the fine solemn poet, were growing together.'

Dylan Thomas has been regarded as a double, if not a 'split' personality. There was his public face and public antics, the personality of a man who liked to be the centre of attention in a bar and who was a self-conscious entertainer; and there was the obscure poet. The public aspect of Thomas can be appreciated from his prose-work *Portrait of the Artist as a Young Dog* (the title adapted from James Joyce's *Portrait of the Artist as a Young Man*). Undoubtedly Dylan Thomas liked to regard himself as a 'young dog'; it was a public image which he wanted to foster and did foster. *Portrait of the Artist as a Young Dog* is a collection of both funny and pathetic prose-pieces which were influenced in their style and outlook by French 'Surrealism' and 'Dadaism'. The book was published in 1940; a previous volume, *The Map of Love*, had been published in the previous year; it contained both prose-pieces and poems. The prose-pieces in this volume are 'semi-surrealist' in their superficial incoherence, their reliance on shock-tactics and the cruelty or obscenity, or both, of much of their imagery. They are failures on the whole, artistically, but they have a real relation to the total pattern of Dylan Thomas's work. They are his *pièces noires*, the pieces in which he accepts evil: they are one side of a medal of which the other side is Thomas's later celebration of innocence, and the benignity of the Reverend Eli Jenkins. In writing these pieces, Thomas was grappling with, and apparently succeeding in absorbing and overcoming, what the Jungians call the 'Shadow' (G. S. Fraser, *Dylan Thomas*, p. 18).

It is therefore suggested that the student should read some of Dylan Thomas's earlier work before turning to *Under Milk Wood*: he should perhaps read *Portrait of the Artist as a Young Dog* and *Adventures in the Skin Trade* first, then the prose-passages of *The Map of Love*, then some of the poems from *Collected Poems*.* It must be remembered that although *Under Milk Wood* was *finished* in the USA under pressure, it is on record that the gestation of this play occupied no less than ten years. A short BBC talk entitled *Quite Early One Morning* contains the essential germ of the play. Observant readers of *Under Milk Wood* will find other echoes from earlier works.

7 'Under Milk Wood'

A general appreciation

A brief history of the writing of this play is given in the 'Preface' by Daniel Jones. The short description of a small Welsh seaside town, in *Quite Early One Morning*, was the starting-point, and this short piece is closely related to the play.

Daniel Jones regards the publication of Dylan Thomas's *Collected Poems* in 1952 as the end of one phase of his literary development. We are told that *Under Milk Wood* grew by 'a slow and natural process'. Daniel Jones refers to the fact that Dylan Thomas had lived in the small seaside town of Laugharne in South Wales, and in New Quay, and that 'there is no doubt that he absorbed the *spirit of these places* and, through imgination and insight, the spirit of all other places like them'. *Under Milk Wood* must, however, not be regarded as a transcript of Laugharne or any other place; on the other hand, it is just as wrong to go to the other extreme with David Holbrook (see Chapter 9 of *Llareggub Revisited*) and regard the Llaregyb of the play simply as 'a kind of Toy Town' – the toy-town of Thomas's childhood. Holbrook writes, 'The place itself bears no relationship to modern Wales, either in village or in town', and 'the effect of the stylization of the piece is to make the world a pretend-place, with pretend-relationships, such as children play, with no morality or reality to impinge'.

It is not altogether correct to regard 1952 as constituting a break, or to suggest that *Under Milk Wood* is part of a new, less personal, more public phase of development. Anyone who reads Dylan Thomas's *Collected Poems* and his prose-works will catch quite a number of echoes from them in *Under Milk Wood*, and there is no doubt that the roots of this play go back

* Some of these were recorded by Dylan Thomas on Caedmon Literary Series, Reading Vol. I (TC 1002); Reading Vol. II (TC 1018); and Reading Vol. III (TC 1043).

deeply into the poet's own experience, which is utilized in a compressed and caricatured form. It is obvious that different persons will react very differently to the play. The longest analysis of it (some forty pages) is by David Holbrook in *Llareggub Revisited*, an analysis which is extremely critical and derogatory, and not a little sanctimonious. Undoubtedly David Holbrook has some interesting and subtle comments to make, but he certainly has not said the last word on the subject. Another critic, G. S. Fraser (in *Dylan Thomas*, London, 1957), wrote that in *Under Milk Wood*, which was Dylan Thomas's last completed work, there is evidence of 'the warmth of his personality, his zest in every kind of human oddity, his love for his fellow-men', and in this play, 'more than in any other prose-work of his, he managed to combine his prose-gift for humorous fantasy, based upon realistic observation [NB] with his poetic gift for piled-up richness of evocative language'.

David Holbrook will have none of this: Thomas's use of the rural scene is 'playfully contemptuous' – 'the attitude of the weekender from sophisticated London, his country people toys in a model farmyard, providing an entertainment which is flattering to those playing with it'. The work reinforces in us an 'infantile detachment from reality'. Holbrook is equally severe on Dylan Thomas's 'poetic gift': thus he talks about the 'tedious' and 'breathless verbal pattern', and even when he grudgingly admits that the play 'may be said to have' comedy and linguistic exuberance, yet even those are 'derived rather from Joyce, often as quite direct borrowings, rather than rooted in any Rabelaisian vitality or Johnsonian irony that seeks to "correct manners" by the laying bare of human self-deluding pretensions'. Holbrook would not, in fact, rate it higher than a comic radio entertainment 'which may be acceptable and even remarkable', but which, 'as art, takes us nowhere, and merely flatters the suburban prejudices'.

In trying to account for the popularity of *Under Milk Wood* Holbrook finds the reasons in the fact that the play is 'essentially cruel and untender and full of seamy hints, obscenities'. In the play he finds 'no moral strength, no compassion, and so no real drama'. It is 'hard, cruel and childishly dirty about sex'. Even its language is not lively: he admits that there are some 'cleverly turned' phrases, but many are 'clichés of journalistic writing'. It is, fundamentally, Holbrook goes on to say, 'the same kind of external handling of language to no purpose found in the worst kind of "clever" advertisement'. There are also 'many phrases which are quite meaningless', e.g. *quiet as a domino*, *the muffled middle*, which are, presumably, the 'poetic' phrases 'if only because we cannot understand them'. His so-called 'vitality' is 'really an abrogation of control over language, so that communication breaks down in a scattered plethora of random expression as merely funny as a child's random babble'; his collections of images 'appear unrelated and unco-ordinated'.

Such then, is *one* critic's reaction, who also accuses Dylan Thomas of 'lack of moral control' and 'lacking the essential compassion of the true artist'. It is recommended strongly that the student should read this essay by David Holbrook, but he must make up his own mind as to whether such extreme positions are tenable.

To return to *Quite Early One Morning*: this proved to be a successful piece when broadcast, and Dylan Thomas determined to write a larger work against the same background (see 'Preface', pp. vi and vii). It is interesting to learn from Daniel Jones that Dylan Thomas began working on this new idea when 'once more settled in his house overlooking Laugharne Estuary'. The first completed part of the play was entitled *Llaregyb*, *a Piece for Radio Perhaps*, and appeared in the Roman publication *Botteghe Oscure* in 1952. The present title was adopted before Thomas's third visit to the USA in 1953. Thomas thought of it first as a 'kind of play for voices' and it 'was to be a dramatic poem on the life of a Welsh village very much like Laugharne. It would have no conventional dramatic continuity, but would consist of an interweaving of many voices, with the strong central voice of a narrator to supply the unities of time, place and situation' (J. M. Brinnin, *Dylan Thomas in America*, p. 103).

Preferably, the play should be read once or twice before the recording is heard, so that the listener, knowing the text, can devote his full attention to its performance. There are some exquisite poetic effects which a casual reader might easily miss, and which are indicated in these notes. No doubt it is easy to find fault with Dylan Thomas as a poet; his range is rather narrow and his technical devices tend to degenerate into tricks. Yet a hard core of unmistakable poetry remains. G. S. Fraser has referred in his study of *Dylan Thomas* to the 'massive emotional directness' that comes across in spite of the intellectual difficulty of many of his poems and their puzzling details, but he points out that 'Thomas's obscurity is not that of a loose and vague but of an extremely packed writer', which leads sometimes to congestion. Yet 'at the heart of his poetic response to experience there is a baffling simplicity'. The present writer first read Dylan Thomas (*18 Poems*) in 1936 and subscribes to the above views. It is shown that Dylan Thomas worked very slowly and painstakingly, using a separate sheet for variations on a single line of a poem, so that a complete poem would eventually emerge from a sheaf of such notes. Little wonder, then, that the meaning is often, at first sight, rather opaque.

G. S. Fraseer is also at pains to stress that Thomas's 'Welshness' is an integral part of his make-up. 'He never spoke or understood the Welsh language, and he very early taught himself to speak English not with slight Welsh sing-song, but with what he himself described mockingly as a "cut-glass accent". He disliked Welsh nationalism and, indeed, all types of nationalism, but Wales remained to him home. His knowledge of the Bible, and his fundamentally religious – emotionally rather than intellectually religious – attitude to life were typically Welsh, his bohemianism was partly a re-action against the puritanism of much of middle-class Welsh life. His sense of verbal music, his feeling for the intricate verbal interplay of vowel and consonant, and also, in prose and conversation, his love of the extravagant phrase and witty exaggeration were Welsh. He was un-English also in his universal gregariousness, his unwillingness to make social discriminations, his complete lack of class-consciousness' (G. S. Fraser's *Dylan Thomas*, pp. 8–9).

It is important to remember that Dylan Thomas conceived *Under Milk Wood* as a 'dramatic poem': the emphasis is on *poem*, and much of the appeal of this work lies in the use of language. Many of the linguistic effects will not be obvious to a casual reader. Some of these effects are pointed out in the following notes, and it is interesting to observe that, although Dylan Thomas did not speak Welsh, he obviously knew something about Welsh prosody, since examples of the Welsh technique of *cynghanedd* are found in the play, e.g. p. 31, kettles – cats – kitchen (ket – cat – kit). Internal rhymes and half-rhymes and alliteration are frequent, and the fact that Dylan Thomas did not make this verbal music 'naturally', but rather deliberately, is illustrated by his own use of the word 'intricate', e.g. 'He intricately rhymes' (*Under Milk Wood*,

p. 20) and 'I, in my intricate image ...' (*Collected Poems*, p. 35).

The reader must decide for himself whether Dylan Thomas 'turned poetry back to a *vieux jeu* of shabby, aesthetic verbalising' (Holbrook).

Note: The title of this play *Under Milk Wood* has never been explained. Apparently it was suggested quite 'spontaneously' after Brinnin had said that he might find a better title than *Llareggub Hill*. Dylan Thomas replied that the joke in the latter title was a 'small and childish one and that the Welsh-looking word itself would be "too thick and forbidding to attract American audiences"'. ' "What about *Under Milk Wood*?" he said, and I said "Fine", and the new work was christened on the spot' (*Dylan Thomas in America*, p. 152). It might well be a schoolboys' name for a lovers' wood, and there is a possible clue in Dylan Thomas's poem 'In the white giant's thigh' (*Collected Poems*, p. 176):

> '. . . or gay with any one
> Young as they in the after milking moonlight lay
> Under the lighted shapes of faith and their moonshade
> Petticoats galed high. . . .'

(For another note on the title see p. 49.)

8 'A play for voices'

In the autumn of 1953 Thomas made his fourth journey to the United States. While he was in New York he took part in a reading of *Under Milk Wood*. It was highly successful, as it was when it was later broadcast by the BBC.

It is sub-titled 'A Play for Voices'. As a radio play it is extremely successful, but it remains a radio play. As John Davenport has said (*Dylan Thomas: The Legend and the Poet*, ed. Tedlock, p. 80), Thomas 'was pleased with *Milk Wood* but deeply dissatisfied that he had been unable to carry out the original scheme from which it had sprung. This was abandoned because he was incapable of dramatic structure. It is the fault of his film scripts, which are more remarkable for the quality of the dialogue than for anything else.'

David Holbrook in his *Llareggub Revisited* also attacks the play. '*Under Milk Wood* has no shape, except what it borrows from *Ulysses*, both in the style of its fantastic dialogue, its pace and in the time-structure of the piece. Essentially it remains episodic reportage, without dramatic progression, without the thesis, antithesis and synthesis of enacted moral argument. It merely registers events as they happen – which is even a fault of its parent . . .' (p. 239).

Daniel Jones, in the Preface to *Under Milk Wood*, describes it as a new departure, a literary development whereby 'he intended to turn from the *strictly personal* type of poetry to a *more public* form of expression, and to large-scale dramatic works in particular, where there would be scope for all his versatility, for his gifts of humour and characterization as well as his genius for poetry' (editor's italics).

Under Milk Wood gives us a cross-section of life in a small Welsh seaside village, from the middle of one night in Spring to the next night. It uses two commentators and numerous voices. The events of this Spring day are recounted by a kind of 'dramatized gossip'. There is no main action, only episodes.

David Holbrook says that the place 'bears no relationship to modern Wales, either in village or town. . . . It is rather the toy-town of Thomas's childhood.' It seems, however, fair to assume that the original model was Laugharne, which lies on an estuary of Carmarthen Bay. Thomas gives us a vivid picture of the setting (p. 24). We learn that the population is less than five hundred, and there are three main streets and a few narrow by-lanes and scattered farmsteads. It is a 'small, decaying water-place', with a 'little fishing harbour' and a man street, called Coronation Street, consisting of 'humble, two-storied houses, many of which attempt to achieve some measure of gaiety by prinking* themselves out in crude colours and the liberal use of pinkwash, though there are remaining a few eighteenth-century houses of more pretension if, on the whole, in a sad state of disrepair'. At the beginning of the play (p. 1) there is a reference to the 'webfoot cockle-women', and in Laugharne there is a 'Flemish colony of cockle-gatherers'.† Laugharne has a public-house, *The Three Mariners*, and Llaregyb has *The Sailors Arms*.

The play has a balanced structure (see Structure of the Play) but there is no main action, only episodes, e.g.

* *prink*, to make oneself spruce, dress oneself up.
† See Augustus John in *Dylan Thomas: The Legend and the Poet*, p. 27.

i) Captain Cat, a blind sea-captain, dreams of his long-drowned mates and recalls his happiness with Rosie Probert.

ii) Mis Price, dressmaker and shopkeeper, dreams of Mr Mog Edwards, the draper who is courting her.

iii) Jack Black, the cobbler, dreams of driving out sin, and goes into the wood to castigate the sinning lovers.

iv) Evans, the undertaker, dreams of his childhood when he stole buns.

v) Mr Waldo dreams of his mother, his dead wife, and other women.

vi) Mrs Ogmore-Pritchard dreams of her two dead husbands, whom she has killed by hygiene.

vii) The milkman dreams of emptying his milk in the river.

viii) The policeman uses his helmet as a chamber-pot.

xi) Mr Willy Nilly, the postman, knocks on Mrs Willy Nilly's back in bed.

David Holbrook finds all this derivative from James Joyce's novel *Ulysses*. 'We have a similar use of characters' dreams, and, apparently, a similar investigation beneath the surface of outward appearance into people's motives and compelling inward drives as we have in Joyce.' Holbrook thinks that 'in the light of the deeper moral functions of art, *Under Milk Wood* is trivial'. It also 'reinforces untenderness. It is a cruel work, inviting our cruel laughter. We need to understand love better – *Under Milk Wood* disguises and confuses.' All that this critic will admit is that *Under Milk Wood* has 'comedy and linguistic exuberance', though even these are often borrowed directly from Joyce. Holbrook concludes: 'Sex, boozing, eccentricity, cruelty, dirty behaviour are enhanced by the implicit background of suburban respectability, the interest lying in the daring naughtiness of their revelation. The norms, or the positives of living, as expressed by the potentialities of human love, are absent; all is denigrated. Sometimes the denigration is relieved by humour, but only sometimes. And on the whole the breathless verbal patter is tedious. . . . *Under Milk Wood* would not have had its popular success were it not essentially cruel and untender, and full of seamy hints, obscenities' (*Llareggub Revisited*, p. 201). He later says (p. 201): 'There is no moral strength in *Under Milk Wood*, but hence no compassion, and so no real drama.'

9 Under Milk Wood

By Dylan Thomas
(First produced in England at the New Theatre, London, on Thursday, 20 September 1956.)

Characters in order of their appearance

Onlooker	Myfanwy Price	3rd Neighbour
Captain Cat	Mog Edwards	4th Neighbour
1st Drowned	Jack Black	Little Boy Waldo
2nd Drowned	Mr Waldo	Matti Richards
Rosie Probert	Waldo's Mother	Matti's Mother
3rd Drowned	Waldo's Wife	The Rev Eli Jenkins
4th Drowned	1st Neighbour	Mrs Ogmore-Pritchard
5th Drowned	2nd Neighbour	Mr Ogmore
Mr Pritchard	Butcher Beynon	Our Sal
Gossamer Beynon	Mr Pugh	Nasty Humphrey
Organ Morgan	Mrs Pugh	Billy Swansea
Mrs Organ Morgan	Mary Ann Sailors	One of Mr Waldo's
Utah Watkins	Dai Bread	Jackie with the Sniff
Mrs Utah Watkins	Polly Garter	1st Woman
Willy Nilly	Nogood Boyo	2nd Woman
Mrs Willy Nilly	Lord Cut-Glass	3rd Woman
P.C. Attila Rees	The Guide Book	4th Woman
Sinbad	Mrs Dai Bread One	Evans the Death
Lily Smalls	Mrs Dai Bread Two	Fishermen
Mae Rose Cottage	Mrs Cherry Owen	Gwenny
Bessie Bighead	Mrs Beynon	Child
Ocky Milkman	Maggie Richards	Mother
Cherry Owen	Ricky Rees	

The action of the play, which in this production was in Two Acts, takes place in Llaregyb in the Spring.

10 The structure of the play

In *Under Milk Wood* there is no conventional division into Acts and Scenes. Nevertheless, there are certain natural breaks, corresponding to time divisions, which divide the play into four portions of almost equal length. The play gives us a cross-section of life in the village over a period of twenty-four hours, as follows:

i) **Night,** pp. 1–22.
   This Section begins, 'It is spring, moonless night in the small town ... all the people of the lulled and dumbfound

town are sleeping now'. The Section ends with the speech of Lord Cut-Glass on p. 22, 'Tick tock tick tock tick tock tick tock'.

ii) **Dawn and early morning,** pp. 22–24.

This Section begins, 'Time passes. Listen. Time passes. An owl flies home past Bethesda, to a chapel in an oak. And the dawn inches up ... you can see all the town below you sleeping in the first of the dawn ... (p. 22) ... The principality of the sky lightens now, over our green hill, into spring morning larked and crowed and belling' (bottom of p. 23). On p. 36 the time is 9 o'clock, for the school bell rings. The Section ends on p. 44, when the Second Voice informs us that 'the town's half over with its morning. The morning's busy as bees.'

iii) **Late morning and afternoon,** pp. 44–66.

The morning ends on p. 56, when the First Voice informs us that 'the morning school is over'. On p. 66 we are told that 'The sunny slow lulling afternoon yawns and moons through the dozy town'.

iv) **Late afternoon, dusk and night,** pp. 66–86.

On p. 73 we are informed by the Second Voice that 'The afternoon buzzes like lazy bees round the flowers round Mae Rose Cottage', but near the bottom of p. 76, 'Now the town is dusk. Each cobble, donkey, goose and gooseberry street is a thoroughfare of dusk. .... Llaregyb is the capital of dusk.' On p. 78 the Second Voice informs us that we are still 'in the dusking town' and 'sundown' is indicated in the poem of the Rev Eli Jenkins on p. 79. On p. 81 the First Voice tells us that 'Dusk is drowned for ever until tomorrow. It is all at once night now.' The time-sequence is completed at the end of the play, p. 86, when 'the suddenly wind-shaken wood springs awake for the *second* dark time this one Spring day' (editor's italics).

For the purpose of analysis and comment the play will be divided into the above four Sections or 'Acts':

'Act I' is introduced by the First Voice, supported by the Second Voice, and switches back to the First Voice, 'In Donkey Street, so furred with sleep ...'.

'Act II' is also introduced by the First Voice. Now that it is dawn it is convenient to give a description of the village, and on p. 23, following the First Voice, is the Voice of the Guide Book. The Section ends with the Second Voice.

'Act III' is introduced by the First Voice showing us the town fully awake – 'the clip clop of horses on the sunhoneyed cobbles of the humming streets, hammering of horse-shoes, gobble quack and cackle'. The Section ends with the Second Voice and Polly Garter.

'Act IV' is introduced by the First Voice and ends with the First Voice.

The play thus appears to be constructed according to a symmetrical plan. Daniel Jones in his introduction to the Dent edition, page vi, points out that Thomas's *Quite Early One Morning* is closely related to *Under Milk Wood*, since it has the same time-sequence, though limited to the hours of a winter's morning: 'we hear the dreams of the sleeping town and see the sleepers getting up and going about their business'. The unities of time and place are observed: the play occupies a period of twenty-four hours and the action takes place wholly in Llaregyb.

(It is interesting to note that when *Under Milk Wood* was first performed at the New Theatre, London (20 September 1956), it was divided into *two* Acts.)

Characters of the play

There are roughly 27 male characters and 36 female characters, in addition to the two anonymous male narrators. The latter – First and Second Voices – and Captain Cat, have the main 'parts'.

Characters in 'Act I'

First Voice	Little Boy Waldo	Lily Smalls
Second Voice	The Four Neighbours	Mae Rose Cottage
The Five Drowned	Mrs Ogmore-Pritchard	Butcher Beynon
Captain Cat	Mr Ogmore	The Rev Eli Jenkins
Rosie Probert	Mr Pritchard	Mr Pugh
Mog Edwards	Gossamer Beynon	Mrs Organ Morgan
Myfanwy Price	Organ Morgan	Mary Ann Sailors
Jack Black	Utah Watkins	Dai Bread
Mr Waldo's Mother	Mrs Utah Watkins	Polly Garter
Mr Waldo	Ocky Milkman	Nogood Boyo
Waldo's Wife	Mrs Willy Nilly	Lord Cut-Glass

Characters in 'Act II'

First Voice	Voice of a Guidebook	Lily Smalls
Second Voice	The Rev Eli Jenkins	Mrs Beynon
Mr Pugh	Nogood Boyo	Cherry Owen

Mrs Pugh	Miss Price	Mr Beynon
Mary Ann Sailors	Polly Garter	Sinbad
Dai Bread	Willy Nilly	Old Man
Mrs Dai Bread One	Mrs Willy Nilly	Mog Edwards
Mrs Dai Bread Two	Captain Cat	Mrs Ogmore-Pritchard
Lord Cut-Glass	Mrs Cherry Owen	Mr Waldo

Characters in 'Act III'

First Voice	Mrs Willy Nilly	Three Boys
Second Voice	Mog Edwards	Girl
The Four Women	Fisherman	Sinbad Sailors (hitherto
Mrs Organ Morgan	Mrs Dai Bread One	known as Sinbad)
Evans the Death	Mrs Dai Bread Two	Mrs Pugh
Gossamer Beynon	Polly Garter	Mr Pugh
Jack Black	The Rev Eli Jenkins	Organ Morgan
Captain Cat	Mr Waldo	
Mary Ann Sailors	Girls' Voices	

Characters in 'Act IV'

First Voice	The Rev Eli Jenkins	Sinbad Sailors
Second Voice	Utah Watkins	First and Second
Mrs Pugh	Bessie Bighead	Woman
Mr Pugh	Mr Pritchard	Mr Waldo
Rosie Probert	Mr Ogmore	First and Third
Captain Cat	Mrs Ogmore-	Drowned
Child	Pritchard	Organ Morgan
Nogood Boyo	Jack Black	Myfanwy Price
Mrs Dai Bread Two	Cherry Owen	Mog Edwards
Mae Rose Cottage	Mrs Cherry Owen	Polly Garter

11 The first and second voices

This is Llaregyb Hill, ... and from this circle of stones you can see all the town below. ...

The major part of this play is taken up by the First Voice, who is the chief commentator and may be regarded as the poet himself. (In the first reading of the play in 1953 Dylan Thomas himself read the parts of the First Voice and the Rev Eli Jenkins.) The two Voices help to give some continuity to the play in its progression round the clock, and share this central vantage-point with Captain Cat.

The First Voice is heard nearly ninety times in the course of the play, and introduces the following 'Acts' and sections:

'Act I', night (p. 1) until dawn.
'Act II', dawn (p. 22) until mid-morning.
'Act III', mid-morning (p. 44) until early afternoon.

'Act IV', late afternoon (p. 66) until late evening. Recommencement of cycle: ('The thin night darkens') p. 86.

The above parts are termed 'Acts' in these Notes. The almost mathematically exact division of the play into these four 'Acts' is worthy of note.

The opening speech of First Voice is the longest in the play, occupying over seventy lines of text. The scene is set: 'spring, mooonless night in the small town, starless and bible-black'.

Under Milk Wood. The title of this play was apparently suggested by Dylan Thomas on the spur of the moment, and no explanation was ever given of it. Yet it is safe to say that nothing ever came to Dylan Thomas on the spur of the moment. The wood is introduced by the First Voice at the very beginning of the play ('the hunched, courters'-and-rabbits' wood') and also takes up most of the very last speech in the play ('The Wood, whose every tree-foot's cloven in the black glad sight of the hunters of lovers . . .'). Milk Wood is the haunt of lovers. The word *milkwood* (written as one word) means any of several trees or shrubs that secrete abundant latex (see *Webster's Third New International Dictionary*, 1961). There might also be a play on the word *milkweed* (certain British wild plants with a milky juice) and *milkwort* (a plant formerly supposed to increase the milk of wet-nurses). Another explanation may be the white farmhouses strewn among the green trees of Llaregyb Hill (see p. 37 of the text).

Page 1, **to begin at the beginning** The play begins and ends with night, covering a span of twenty-four hours. Is this an echo of T. S. Eliot's *In my End is my Beginning*?

bible-black 'Black' is one of the poet's favourite adjectives − see also p. 2, '*black*, dab-filled sea'; '*bombazine black*' and 'flying like *black* flour'; p. 1, 'sloeblack, slow, black, crowblack'; p. 3, 'the silent *black* bandaged night'; p. 7, 'the bible-*black* airless attic'. This adjective is also frequently used in Dylan Thomas's poems, e.g.

> The horizontal cross-bones of Abaddon,
> Yon by the cavern over the *black* stairs;

and For, oh, my soul found a Sunday wife
> In the coal-*black* sky . . . (*Lament*)

and Innocence sweetens my last *black* breath (*Lament*)

and Cawing from their *black* bethels soaring (*In Country Sleep*).

Daniel Jones has said (*Dylan Thomas: The Legend and the Poet*, p. 17) that he and Thomas used to have word-obsessions − 'everything at one time was little or white'.

Dylan Thomas was the grandson of a Welsh preacher, and in his poems the pervading presence of the Bible is felt. The preacher in Wales is associated with a puritanical outlook, 'a code that Thomas mocked and feared' (Cecil Price in *Dylan Thomas: The Legend and the Poet*, p. 19). Francis Scarfe, in the same book (p. 99) says that the fervency of the Biblical references is due to the fact that 'the Bible appears as a cruel and crazy legend, as seen through the childish memories of hot-gospelling and the diabolical grimace of the Welsh Bethel'. *Bible-black* in this context evokes a cruel and hostile universe ('starless and bible-black') and terrifying punishments for sinners. Even when dawn breaks (p. 24) the Rev Eli Jenkins gropes out of bed into his preacher's *black*. Similarly (p. 79) it is Jack *Black* who prepares 'to meet his Satan in the Wood'.

It seems, then, that this adjective also became obsessional with Dylan Thomas. In 'A Prospect of the Sea'* we have '*blackbirds*'; 'the *black*, triangular flight of birds'; 'ten *black* scissor-blades'; and 'eyes that were sea-blue with *black* lashes'. In 'The Visitor' (in the same volume), Dylan Thomas says of the birds that they have 'white and *black* in their whistling'; in 'The Followers' we read of the 'big *black* circular birds of their umbrellas', and 'reprobate grannies in dustbin *black*'. In 'The Lemon' we read that 'a storm came up, *black*-bodied', and in 'The Orchard' we read of 'the reverend madmen in the *Black* Book of Llareggub', as well as the '*black* lots', 'the *black* birds', 'the *blackened* grass', 'the *black*-nailed and warning fingers', and 'a *black* flower-bed'. A sinister note of impending doom runs through these examples. (It is worth noting that the name Llareggub was first used in 'The Orchard'.)

courters' and rabbits' wood Milk Wood is a favourite haunt of courting couples.

sloeblack, slow, black, crowblack Reminiscent of both G. M. Hopkins and James Joyce. A *sloe* is a small, bluish-black wild plum. The rhythm of this phrase suggests the inexorable swell of the sea.

fishingboat-bobbing sea cf. 'a bursting sea with bottleneck boats' (*Collected Poems*, p. 132).

the snouting, velvet dingles A species of jugglery characteristic of the poet. cf. also 'dogs in the wetnosed yards' (p. 2) and 'pig-loving sun' (p. 67).

---

* This story and the other ones mentioned are to be found in the collection entitled *A Prospect of the Sea*.

the shops in mourning i.e. covered with (?black) shutters. *Alliteration* **'Welfare Hall in widows weeds.'**

dumbfound The correct past participle of this verb is *dumbfounded* (struck dumb, nonplussed). Here it means that the people are unable to speak, because they are asleep.

First Voice now indicates some of the people who live in the village – babies, farmers, fishers, tradesmen and pensioners, cobbler and so on.

The boys are dreaming wicked or of the bucking ranches of the night David Holbrook (*Llareggub Revisited*, p. 209) regards this as 'school-boyish naughty talk' which 'is not quite obscene, but it sounds obscene'. The noun *buck* refers to the male of the rabbit, hare, deer, etc.; and the verb *to buck* (of horse) means to jump vertically with arched back and feet drawn together.

the organplaying wood This might have, as Holbrook thinks, 'a salacious double meaning'. Dylan Thomas might also have had in mind Baudelaire's famous poem *Correspondances*:

La Nature est un temple ou de vivants piliers
Laissent parfois sortir de confuses paroles.

The association is between tree-trunks and pillars of a temple, or trees and organ-pipes, as suggested in the second stanza of *Correspondances*:

Comme de long échos qui de loir se confondent
Dans une ténébreuse et profonde unité.

anthracite statues The black, hard outlines of the shapes of horses. *Anthracite* is the non-bituminous kind of coal mined chiefly in South Wales.

Page 2, **'darkest-before-dawn minutely dewgrazed stir of the black, dab-filled sea'** *Consonantal pattern d - b - d, d - b - d.* A *dab* is a kind of flat-fish.

Llaregyb Previously spelt (in Dylan Thomas's *A Prospect of the Sea*) Llareggub (=an oath spelt backwards).

bombazine (=bombasine), twilled dress material of worsted with silk or cotton, used for mourning.

choker something worn about the throat; a wide neckcloth, cravat or collar with high wings.

four-ale ale sold at 4d a quart in former times.

nannygoats female goats.

cockled cobbles cobbles littered with cockle-shells or convex and ribbed like cockle-shells.

Coronation Street Street built (or re-named) at the time of the coronation of Edward VII or George V.

Page 3, **Time passes. Listen. Time passes. Come closer now.**
Holbrook finds here an echo of T. S. Eliot's *East Coker*

> If you do not come too close, if you do not come too close,
> On a summer midnight. . . .

dicky-bird watching pictures The order given by early
photographers to 'watch the dicky-bird' in order to make their
clients sit still, often produced 'wooden' portraits. Dylan Thomas
uses this word in *A Portrait of the Artist as a Young Dog* and in
Adventures in the Skin Trade.

The Second Voice has a much less important part to play
than the First Voice, sometimes acting as an *alter ego* to the
First Voice, or being used to add a note of variety to the play.
The first appearance of the Second Voice is to introduce
himself by taking over the last few lines of the First Voice's
speech.

the Davy dark The bottom of the sea ('Davy Jones's Locker').
nibble him down to his wishbone This speech is described by
Holbrook as an example of 'neurotic writing' which the reader
may fail to notice because the poet 'has reduced our response to
language' by his 'daft effervescence'. The speech is regarded as
an example of Dylan Thomas's preoccupation with 'corpses and
decay, an obsession always mixed with strong sexual overtones'
(see *Llareggub Revisited*, p. 210). *Wishbone* here refers to the male
genital organs (cf. the use of '*nibble*' in *Collected Poems*, p. 37).
'This keen stimulation of morbid necrophilia is a sick element in
Thomas's writing.' In case the reader may think that Holbrook
is taking it all too seriously, the latter points out that on p. 71
Dylan Thomas 'attempts to write his most serious lines':

> Remember her
> She is forgetting,
> The earth which filled her mouth
> Is vanishing from her.
> Remember me,
> I have forgotten you,
> I am going into the darkness of the darkness for ever.
> I have forgotten that I was ever born.

The First Voice comes in again at the end of Captain Cat's
speech on p. 6, introducing us to Cockle Row and Miss Price.
Then follow three examples of the Second Voice, taking over
an unfinished speech from the First Voice, a device which

Dylan Thomas may have used to lessen the monotony of a single commentator.

Page 6. *Alliteration* **blowlamps - low - lonely - loving** Miss Price is dreaming of her lover, Mr Mog Edwards, who, in her dream, is transmuted from an ordinary draper into a resplendent romantic figure. It seems to be the aim of the poet throughout the play to show us persons who, in one way or another, are all unhappy, dissatisfied, emotionally unbalanced. Miss Price is a 'lonely' soul, in need of human love ('hotwaterbottled'). In her dream Mog Edwards tells her to throw away her 'little bedsocks' and 'Welsh wool knitted jacket', and then he will 'warm the sheets like an electric toaster', and lie by her side 'like the Sunday roast' (p. 7).

Page 7. **before the mice gnaw at your bottom drawer** The basic reference here is to the bottom drawer in which a bride-to-be collects her household linen. Once again, however, there is the sexual *double-entendre* – 'gnaw', 'bottom', 'drawer'. It is very unlikely that Dylan Thomas made a serious study of Freud, but he was aware of the symbolism of dreams as explained by Freud.

The First Voice continues his task of introducing us to the village and its inhabitants, reminding us that it is still night. We are then introduced to Jack Black, another character whose dream is sexual in nature. This time, however, instead of yielding to the dream images, Jack Black is combating them. He had, indeed, taken precautions before going to sleep, tying his night shirt to his ankles with elastic. He dreams 'alone and savagely' that he is an appointed guardian of morals – 'chasing the naughty couples down the grassgreen gooseberried double bed of the wood, flogging the tosspots in the spit-and-sawdust, driving out the bare bold girls from the sixpenny hops of his nightmares'.

the dark night seesawing like a sea Seesawing refers to the rhythm of the sexual act. The word is also used in Dylan Thomas's poem 'Lament' (*Collected Poems*, p. 174):

When I was a windy boy and a bit
And the black spit of the chapel fold,
(Sighed the old ramrod, dying of women),
I tiptoed shy in the gooseberry wood,
The rude owl cried like a telltale tit,
I skipped in a blush as the big girls rolled
Ninepin down on the donkeys' common,
And on seesaw Sunday nights I wooed
Whoever I would with my wicked eyes.

David Holbrook says of this poem that its attitude to sexual love is the same as that in *Under Milk Wood*. ' "Lament" is a last attempt to justify, cynically, the life of "sin" – that sin which he fiercely asserts against a world whose reality he cannot accept, in order to force the world to accept him as still-a-child. . . . "Lament" is no account of the sexual reality – it is a special plea for the kind of anti-life, suicidal, anarchy to which Thomas himself, the child who is unable to grow up, had come: Virtue is deadly' (*Llareggub Revisited*, p. 225).

gooseberried From to 'play gooseberry', i.e. act as chaperon for courting couples.
tosspots boozers.
spit-and-sawdust The cheap bar or vault of the public house.
sixpenny hop Cheap dance held in the village hall

The First Voice then brings in Evans the Death, the undertaker (p. 8), who is described by the Second Voice. Evans is another example of loneliness, a man looking nostalgically back upon a vanished childhood. His mother is also symbolically portrayed as an unhappy woman 'crying out for her lost currants'.

The next character to be introduced by the First Voice is Mr Waldo, another dissatisfied person yearning for the past and his mother (p. 8). The next part of the play (pp. 9–13) is taken up by comments made by the four neighbours on Waldo and his wife. Mrs Waldo is yet another character who is presented as an unhappy, neurotic woman, 'screaming' when she first appears, and terrified of her neighbours' gossiping tongues, but gently dominated by her seventeen-stone husband, described by the neighbours as a drunkard and fornicator. His wife partly represents his mother who, in her turn, was greatly concerned about what the neighbours would say. Mr Waldo has never really grown up; his adult antics are what one would expect from his boyhood record (pp. 11–12).

Page 12. **playing mwchins** The Welsh word 'mochyn' means 'pig' or 'dirty little boy', and probably refers here, since there is a reference to 'in the bushes', to self-abuse, the remedy for which is a good dose of senna-pods and being locked in the dark. A similar word is also used in Dylan Thomas's poem 'Once it was the Colour of Saying' first published in *The Map of Love*, then in *Collected Poems* (p. 89).

> When I whistled with mitching boys through a reservoir park
> Where at night we stoned the cold and cuckoo
> Lovers in the dirt of their leafy beds.

The word here is the dialect word *to mitch*, 'prowl about', 'play truant'.

We see (p. 13) that Waldo had successfully escaped from the clutches of many women, only to be caught eventually by Blodwen Bowen, who became his 'awful wedded wife' (cf. A. P. Herbert's title, *Holy Deadlock*). The humour of Dylan Thomas sometimes tends to be on this adolescent or music-hall level.

The First Voice next introduces Mrs Ogmore-Pritchard (p. 14), 'widow, twice' (see Section on Mrs Ogmore-Pritchard, pp. 52–55). The First Voice continues to introduce characters: Gossamer Beynon, daughter of the butcher (p. 16), but variety is then provided by the Second Voice briefly introducing the next character, Organ Morgan (p. 16). The First Voice quickly takes over again to introduce the cocklers, Mr and Mrs Floyd (who do not appear again in the play), Mr and Mrs Utah Watkins, Ocky Milkman (p. 17) and PC Attila Rees.

Page 18, **the backyard lock-up of his sleep** A reference to the Freudian 'unconscious'. In *New Verse*, October, 1934, Thomas wrote, 'Poetry must drag into the clear-nakedness of light even more of the hidden causes that Freud could realise'; and Francis Scarfe wrote (*Dylan Thomas: The Legend and the Poet*), 'Only a reader of Freud can receive the full impact, which is enormous, of Dylan Thomas's predominantly sexual imagery'.

The First Voice is now assisted by 'A Voice', who is followed by the Second Voice introducing Willy Nilly the Postman and his wife.

The First and Second Voice then alternate (pp. 18–20), introducing respectively Sinbad Sailors (landlord of *The Sailors Arms*), Lily Smalls, Mae Rose Cottage, Bessie Bighead, Mr Beynon and the Reverend Eli Jenkins.

every night of her married life she has been late for school Holbrook comments on this (*Llareggub Revisited*, p. 221): 'a simple and misapplied Freudianism – hinting, with a naughty leer, that you will find, under the surface, people's impulses governed by their childhood sins, you will find in their inward selves dirty dreams and wicked desires'.

a mogul One of the Mohammedan conquerors of India or their descendants; hence, a great personage or autocrat.

Page 19. **Mae, peals off her pink-and-white skin ... raw as an onion ... brilliantined trout** Holbrook refers to Dylan

Thomas's 'playful vigour' which 'can establish a kind of humanity, revealing in its very babbling extravagance an ironic perception of the idiocies of adult antics'. This passage is Thomas's version of 'Joyce's pastiche of Gerty MacDowell's reading matter in the Nausicaa chapter of *Ulysses:* the sexual undertones . . . arise from the unconscious – and they satirise the onanistic intensity of the vision, comically expanded to the grotesque' (*Llareggub Revisited*, p. 197).

The First Voice now introduces the farm servant, Bessie Bighead.

Inspectors of Cruelty Refers to the Inspectors of the RSPCA (Royal Society for the Prevention of Cruelty to Animals).
manchop An excellent 'invention' of the poet. Refers to human flesh, chop being used in both its original meaning and Far Eastern connotation of food in general.

Second Voice now takes over to bring in again Butcher Beynon, then the First and Second Voices alternate. Here is a short interlude of highly alliterative prose, followed by 'camera directions' providing a short change of scene before the remainder of the characters are introduced, mainly by the First Voice: the Reverend Eli Jenkins; the schoolmaster, Mr Pugh; Organ Morgan and his wife; and the innkeeper's daughter, Mary Ann Sailors; Dai Bread; Polly Garter; Nogood Boyo and Lord Cut-Glass.

Page 20, *sound effect* The susurration of the sea is reproduced by the repetition of *s*-sounds: eye**s** and **s**ecrets of the dreamers in the **s**treets rocked to **s**leep by the **s**ea, **s**ee . . .'
Alliteration **t**itbits and **t**opsy-turvies, **b**obs and **b**utton tops, **b**ags and **b**ones.
Bethesda 'House of Mercy'. A public bath in Jerusalem where Christ healed the impotent man. Birkit Israel, situated in Jerusalem, has been identified with it since 1102. Also a town in North Wales, and a common chapel name.
Page 21, **dulcet** sweet to the eye, ear, taste or feelings, e.g. 'dulcet creams' (Milton, *Paradise Lost*, v. 347).
Page 22, **Nogood Boyo** This name is an echo of James Joyce's Blazes Boylan: other names echoing Joyce's ironic use include Sinbad Sailors (from 'Sinbad the Sailor and Tinbad the Tailor'); Mrs Ogmore-Pritchard (the Hon Mrs Mervyn Talboys); the Rev Eli Jenkins (the Rev Mr Haines Love or Father Malachi O'Flynn).
Cut-Glass In *Letters to Vernon Watkins* we read that Dylan Thomas referred to his own cultivated accent as a 'cut-glass accent'.

'Act II' begins on p. 22, and again the First Voice opens the Act: 'Time passes. Listen. Time passes.' This is a repetition of the First Voice's words at the top of p. 3, and helps to effect continuity.

The First Voice, from a vantage-point on Llaregyb Hill, then gives us a panoramic view of the town below 'sleeping in the first of the dawn'.

Note *vowel harmony:* 'lake in the waking haze'.

'farmyards away' Dylan Thomas was fond of inventing new adverbial locutions (cf. *Collected Poems,* the poem 'A Grief Ago').

After the Voice of a Guide Book has provided us with topographical and other details relating to the town, the First Voice again indicates the gradual passage of time: 'The principality of the sky lightens now, over our green hill ...'. Morning is announced by Captain Cat pulling the bell-rope.

Page 24. Note *consonantal patterns:* **'pulls the town hall bell-rope but blind ...'** (p-l, t-l, b-l, bl).

The Second Voice then takes over to show the Reverend Eli Jenkins getting up and performing his 'morning service'. The First Voice resumes (p. 26) to introduce Lily Smalls, Mrs Beynon's servant (her 'treasure'), and Mrs Beynon herself (p. 26), and the First Voice continues, now introducing Mr Pugh and his wife (pp. 27–8). The Second Voice again comes in and helps to indicate the slight passage of time by showing Lily Smalls at her morning chores – her first task is to make the tea, then to clean the front step. The Second Voice continues, now showing us the local policeman, P.C. Attila Rees.

Page 28. Note *partial cynghanedd* **heav(y) – huff**.

The First Voice then introduces the old lady, mother of the landlord of *The Sailors Arms* (p. 29), and we see Organ Morgan at his bedroom window and the noisy gulls which observe the scene below. (The next seven speeches all begin with the word 'Me', the characters speaking for themselves and thus allowing the First and Second Voices to have a brief respite. Dai Bread, Mrs Dai Bread One, Mrs Dai Bread Two, Lord Cut-Glass, Nogood Boyo, Miss Price and Polly Garter.)

Page 30, **'in an old frock-coat belonged ...'** Note omission of relative pronoun 'which'.
Bethesda Jumble The jumble sale held at the chapel.

We are again made aware by the First Voice of the slight passage of time, since we are informed that it is now breakfast-time, and 'frying-pans spit, kettles and cats purr in the kitchen. The town smells of seaweed and breakfast' (p. 31). From this point in the play until the end of 'Act II' the First Voice predominates: the Second Voice takes over briefly on p. 37 and again at the end of the Act.

The First Voice shows us Mary Ann Sailors, Mrs Pugh, Willy Nilly the Postman and Mrs Willy Nilly, the Reverend Eli Jenkins, Lord Cut-Glass, Mr and Mrs Cherry Owen at their various activities. We then move on to Mrs Beynon, Mr Beynon and Lily Smalls. The Beynons keep a butcher's shop in Coronation Street, and they are just having their breakfast. The scene then moves 'up the street' (p. 36) to *The Sailors Arms*, where the landlord, already at this early time, draws himself a pint and drinks his own health. At this point another indication of the passage of time is given by the ringing of the school bell (bottom of p. 36). The Second Voice then takes over (p. 37) and the scene changes to the fishermen and the bay, where Nogood Boyo, in an atheistic mood, says 'I don't know who's up there and I don't care'. It is now time for the shops to open and the First Voice shows us Mr Edwards standing at the door of Manchester House and whispering to himself his love for Miss Price. The school bell is still ringing (p. 38) and further activity in the village is indicated by the First Voice – a car driving to market, full of fowls, and Captain Cat now sitting at his window listening to the sounds of the morning. This 'Act' ends with the Second Voice informing us that 'the town's half over with its morning'.

'Act II' ends with the crowing of a cock, followed by Captain Cat and the Second Voice, then organ music fading into silence.

'Act III' is introduced by the First Voice (p. 44), who gives us a typical piece of Dylan Thomas's poetic prose – 'clip clop of horses on the sunhoneyed cobbles of the humming streets, hammering of horseshoes, gobble quack and cackle, tomtit twitter from the bird-ounced boughs, braying on Donkey Down'. The morning is now well advanced, and the village fully awake and at work. This speech is highly evocative of the sound and movement of the village. 'Bread is baking, pigs are grunting, chop goes the butcher, milk-churns bell, tills ring, sheep cough, dogs shout, saws sing.'

Page 44, boat-bobbing river See note on 'fishingboat-bobbing sea', p. 21.

sanderlings Small sandpipers with mostly grey and white plumage.

beargarden school A beargarden was a place for baiting bears and for other rough pastimes; hence, a rowdy, undisciplined school.

This Act continues with the four Women (there were five in Act I) amusing themselves with scandalous gossip about Mrs Ogmore-Pritchard, Butcher Beynon, Nogood Boyo, Ocky Milkman's wife, Dai Bread and his two wives, Organ Morgan.

Page 45, got a man in Builth Wells Willy Nilly has already brought a letter for Mrs Ogmore-Pritchard (p. 39) from Builth Wells, from 'a gentleman who wants to study birds'.

got a little telescope to look at birds 'Birds' is accepted in the sense of 'girls' by the Third and First Women.

Page 46, you look dead beat An insinuation regarding Mrs Morgan's marital life.

Page 47, it's organ organ all the time with him Another *double-entendre*, referring to Mr Morgan's excessive sexual needs, followed by a typical humorous reply, 'Oh, I'm a martyr to music'.

After this fairly long section of the four Women (pp. 44–7) the First Voice resumes with a reference to the spring scene in Llaregyb. The poet here seems to be enjoying his memories of the village.

snip piece that is snipped off, a fragment.

The Second Voice now takes over, bringing in Evans the Death, Gossamer Beynon and Jack Black. We do not encounter the latter again until the end of the play (p. 79), when he is preparing 'to meet his Satan in the wood'.

he hammers it sternly out Jack Black's hammering symbolizes the driving-out of evil thoughts from his mind.

Page 48, there is no leg ... this shoe Jack Black refuses to let his thoughts dwell on the subject of female flesh.

The beautiful spring weather reminds Captain Cat of the tropics. He thinks of dark-skinned (mulatto) girls.

Parlez-vous, jig-jig, Madam? Jig-jig is a word used internationally by prostitutes in ports.

The First Voice comes in again, showing us the postman steaming open letters in his kitchen.

cynghanedd: the dr**ugg**ed, **be**dr**aggl**ed hens (*dr - g - d, dr - g - d*).
lickerish An obsolete word meaning tempting the appetite (cf. modern German *lecker*): there is also word-play on 'liquorice'.

The voice of Mog Edwards now reads the letter which Willy Nilly has opened, a letter to Myfanwy Price.

Page 49, all dripping wet ... mermaid This follows the same mood of sexual allusion as in 'Act I' (p. 3) – 'jellyfish-slippery'. Also in 'Act I' (p. 4) there is Alfred Pomeroy Jones 'tatooed with mermaids'. The poet is thinking of the tactile sensations that would be associated with such a creature, half-woman, half-fish.

The First Voice continues, showing us Willy-Nilly going out to the latrine at the back of the house, and this provides the Second Voice with a further opportunity (p. 50) of giving us a picture of another corner of the village, the harbour, in the late morning. The water is perfectly calm, but the fishermen pretend that the weather is far too rough for them to go out fishing.

Page 50, heckling 'To heckle' means to catechize severely, especially an election candidate. The word is used here in order to produce the musical alliteration herring – heckling – harbour.
gob spit.
Page 51, draggletail Woman with draggled or untidily trailing skirts. Hardly appropriate here, but an example of Thomas's choice of a word simply for its sound and visual impact.

The Second Voice now shows us Captain Cat, setting words to the rhythm of the children's song.
The First Voice speaks again, recreating the atmosphere of the place.

the music of the Spheres An ethereal harmony which the Pythagoreans supposed to be produced by the vibration of the celestial spheres upon which the stars and planets were thought to move. There is a related doctrine, the *harmony of the spheres*, to the effect that the celestial spheres are separated by intervals corresponding to the relative lengths of strings that produce harmonious tones. Dylan Thomas might also have been thinking of Gustav Holst's suite *The Planets* (Op. 32, 1914–7), which is seven movements, the character of each planet suggesting to him a strongly contrasting mood.

First Voice then shows us Mrs Ogmore-Pritchard and Second Voice the baker's two wives, Mrs Dai Bread One and Mrs Dai Bread Two. The passages which follow (pp. 52–3) are subject to a fierce attack by Holbrook.

the Rustle of Spring Music composed by the Norwegian Christian Sinding (1856–1914). The original title is *Frühingsräuschen*.

The song. It should be noted that the children sing this song, *not* Captain Cat, who merely says the words. Here again, sexual symbolism can be read into the apparently innocuous words. Psycho-analysts first encountered symbolism in their study of dreams but found later that the same symbols and the same interpretation could be discovered in religion, ceremonial, myth and fairy-stories. Symbolism is a form of indirect expression in which there is a mental relation between the symbol and the thing symbolized.

The pages which follow (pp. 52–3) show us Mrs Dai Bread One and Two. Mrs Dai Bread One is crystal-gazing, and the theme of the little man (see previous note on the children's song) is presented – 'a hairy little man with big pink lips', who 'grips his little arms round one of the women'.

Page 52, **wall eye** (Usually spelt as one word or hyphenated.) An eye which turns outward, showing an undue amount of white; a divergent squint: fierce or glaring eyes (from old Norse 'vagl', a beam in the eye). Probably here means 'lustful'.

The First Voice takes over again to show us the Reverend Eli Jenkins on his morning round of visits, and Polly Garter scrubbing the floor for the Mothers' Union Dance. (See section on Polly Garter.) We are again made aware of the passage of time when the First Voice tells us it is midday – 'the morning school is over' and the children rush out into the cobbled street.

Page 56, **forfeiting** playing the game of 'forfeits'.

The children in *Under Milk Wood* are regarded by Holbrook as 'a glimpse at innocence at the undiscriminating attitude to experience for which Thomas himself yearns', he finds 'the role of the children and their "traditional" songs not very profound or interesting' (*Llareggub Revisited*, pp. 229–30). It seems, however, that this section is a simple transcript from Thomas's own childhood.

After this rather long passage of the girls and the boys, the First Voice introduces a scene of movement: the noisy girls delighting in their victory and the 'bully brothers' hooting his nickname (Dirty Dick) after the victim. It is a passage which Dylan Thomas evidently found enjoyment in writing. There is a passage in *Adventures in the Skin Trade*, p. 21, which is reminiscent of this scene: '. . . down went the Girls' School and the long-legged, smiling colts with their black knickers and bows, the hockey-legged girls who laughed behind their hands as they came running through the gates when he passed . . .'.

Page 59, **cawl** broth, gruel (Welsh).
welshcakes A kind of currant cake baked on a griddle.

The Second Voice takes over (p. 60) with a vivid image of the butcher's daughter high-heeling out of school followed by the gaze of the villagers.

Page 60, **bees** Probably from Welsh 'biswn', 'fine linen', 'underclothes', cf. English 'byssus'.
the first mangrowing cock-crow garden The Garden of Eden (cf. also *Collected Poems* – 'Altarwise by Owl-light'; III, and 'Once it was the Colour of Saying').
the Dai-Adamed earth i.e. a world inhabited by primitive Celts.
Page 61, **all cucumber and hooves** sexual symbols.

Holbrook regards these passages on Gossamer Beynon as 'merely obscene suggestiveness' (*Llareggub Revisited*, p. 227). 'The excitement of Dylan Thomas's suggestive passages depends upon the presence of recoil and shame', and Thomas's language (strip her to the nipples, cucumber, etc.) has an autoerotic stimulus.

The First Voice now takes us into the dark dining-room of School House and shows us Mr and Mrs Pugh at table. The next two pages (62–3) are devoted to the latter characters, Mrs Morgan and her husband then occupy the scene until p. 65.

Page 64, **one big bird gulp** Refers to Mrs Morgan whose mouth is as full of fish as a pelican's.
Page 65, **Palestrina** An Italian composer (1525–94) whose works consist mainly of sacred music. In 1571 he was appointed choirmaster at St Peter's, Rome, under Pope Gregory XIII. He composed nearly a hundred masses, hundreds of motets, hymns and litanies.

The First Voice now takes us to Lord Cut-Glass's clock-loud kitchen, in a speech full of subtle rhythms — rhythms which are themselves evocative of the varying movements of different clocks. After this long speech the Second Voice takes over, informing us that the beautiful spring-day is lost on this crazy man, whose thoughts are full of the Day of Judgment.

Page 66, Note *alliteration* Lust — lilt — lather.

lilt Evidently a favourite word of Dylan Thomas, cf. p. 61, 'with never a look or lilt or wriggle'. (cf. *Collected Poems*, page 159, 'Fern Hill'. 'About the lilting house and happy as the grass was green.')

lather cf. 'the green lathered trees' (p. 37).

Armageddon Hill Armageddon is a scene described in the Book of the *Revelation* (xvi, 16), where the Kings of the World are depicted as gathering together for a final battle before the end of the world.

consonantal pattern Double-locked . . . dust-scrabbled (*d - bl - d, d - bl - d*)

This Act ends with Polly Garter singing a snatch of her song.

After a silence the First Voice resumes, indicating that the afternoon is well advanced. Dylan Thomas makes great use of liquid *l*- and *z*-sounds and long vowels ('yawns, moons, dozy, lazy, snooze') to give an impression of the lazy warmth of a late spring day: 'lulling, lolls, laps, idles, sleeping, lap, still, tasselled, bulls, dingles, pillow, wallow, smile, swill, squeal'.

Page 67, **acorned** The acorn is a favourite food of the pig, e.g. in the oak-forests of Portugal.

pig-loving sun A typical-inversion and compression — cf. 'the seal-barking moon' (p. 70).

Mr and Mrs Pugh again appear (last seen on pp. 62–3).

soft-soaping flattering, wheedling.

Doctor Crippen Murderer apprehended, in the company of Ethel Le Neve, on board S.S. *Montrose*. This was the first occasion on which the radio-telephone had been used for such a purpose.

prussic The reference is to the poison prussic acid.

Page 68, **Black Death** The bubonic plague which struck England in 1345 and swept the country, causing widespread death.

stalactite A deposit (calcium carbonate) hanging from the roof or sides of a cavern and resembling an icicle in shape.

The First Voice and Second Voice (pp. 68–71) now introduce the scene of Captain Cat and Rosie Probert.

Page 71, **up the silences and echoes of the passages of the eternal night** This line is reminiscent of both Pascal's statement and Alphonse de Lamartine's famous poem (*Le Lac*) –

> Le Silence éternel de ces vastes espaces m'effraie *(Pascal)*.
> Ainsi, toujours poussés vers de nouveaux rivages,
> Dans la nuit eternelle emportés sans retour *(Lamartine)*.

The child and his mother now make a brief appearance, followed by a view of Nogood Boyo out in the bay.

Page 72, **a nose like strawberries** i.e. pock-marked and with a rosaceous appearance.

bluebagged Formed from the expression 'blue bags' (under the eyes), i.e. with small waves. This could also refer to the 'blue bag' used in washing clothes.

gypsies up his mind's slow eye The gypsies (also gipsies or Romany) are itinerant groups of people who came originally from India. Their typical occupations are horse-dealing, basket-making, fortune-telling. The phrase here means to become excited by one's own visions.

Page 73, **geisha girl** A specially trained female entertainer (*not* a prostitute) in Japan.

kimono From the Japanese kimono, a loose robe tied with a sash and worn as an outer garment by both men and women.

Note *vowel harmony*. 'Sighs, writhes, politely'; and 'uneasy, Eastern, Japanese.'

in a Japanese minute Probably a reference to the Japanese art of self-defence known as *jujitsu* (from Japanese *ju*, yielding, and *jitsu*, art), characterized by rapidity of movement.

The First Voice now brings in the Reverend Eli Jenkins, who, at this moment, is engaged on his life-work, a historical guide and gazetteer of Llaregyb.

Page 74, **undogcollared** The 'dog-collar' is the round collar worn by parsons. To undogcollar, therefore, means to unfrock, to dismiss from a pastoral appointment because of sexual or other misbehaviour.

his little weakness Dalliance with the opposite sex.

Salt Lake Farm A rather forced metaphor. Salt Lake City is the capital of Utah, USA. Its history is intimately bound up with that of the State of Utah and the Mormons. The latter are adherents of a religious body founded by Joseph Smith, who developed an elaborate theology and creed which soon attracted numerous followers. The Mormons' doctrines included polygamy. The idea here is simply that the farmer is surrounded by numerous female animals.

The Second Voice now indicates the passage of time. 'The coming of the end of the Spring day . . .'. The First Voice resumes to tell us something about Bessie Bighead the milk-maid, who figures in the Reverend Eli Jenkins's White Book. Dylan Thomas pays great attention to vowel music and *cynghanedd* in this passage:

Play on long and short i-sounds. Bighead, in, White, will, find, glittering, history, in, until, kissed, light, sing, milk, night, spits, into, sky, life, light, holily, Bessie, milks, slowly.

Cynghanedd Born in a barn; and Curses . . . carthorse.

Indications of the passage of time are now more frequent in order to show the swift descent of night. The Second Voice has already indicated that the end of the day is coming (p. 75); now the First Voice tells us (p. 76) that 'the town is dusk'.

Page 76, **the capital of dusk** The poet's intention here seems to say that this is the most important time of the day to which the inhabitants of Llaregyb look forward.

The First Voice now brings back Mrs Ogmore-Pritchard and her two husbands. Alliteration and vowel-harmony are again found in this passage (pp. 76–7).

Page 77, **glass widow** Play on *grass*-widow; also refers to the cold brittle nature of this woman.
tears where their eyes once were cf. Ariel's song in Shakespeare's *The Tempest*, I. ii,

> Full fathom five thy father lies
> Of his bones are coral made.
> Those are pearls that were his eyes. . . .

The Second Voice again refers to 'the dusking town' and shows us Mae Rose Cottage who is 'still lying in clover' – she has been there since the afternoon (see p. 73). The time has now arrived for the Reverend Eli Jenkins to recite his 'sunset poem'. The First Voice now shows us Jack Black, the self-appointed guardian of morals setting out with torch and Bible to do his nightly rounds ('joyfully' – deriving a vicarious pleasure) of spying on the courting couples in Milk Wood.

Page 79, **sinning dusk** Typical personification.
Gomorrah Sodom and Gomorrah were towns in the lower Jordan valley which were destroyed by fire because of the offensive practice of sodomy (Genesis, XIX. 24).

The First Voice now brings in Cherry Owen, who is off to *The Sailors Arms* for his evening carousal.

Page 81, **open yours** *i.e.* your arms.

The First Voice then indicates that dusk has passed into night, and 'the windy town is a hill of windows'.
The First Voice now gives us a final view of some of the inhabitants and their activities: the babies and the old men being 'bribed and lullabied to sleep', the unmarried girls getting themselves ready for marriage – the Dance of the World (cf. p. 1).

Page 82, note *alliteration* **Lamplit** – **leaning** – **all** – **at** (*la* - *li* - *lea* - *la*); and **wait** – **once** – **wind** – **wolve** – **whistle** (*wai* - *wo* - *wi* - *wo* - *whi*).

The First Voice continues, showing us men of the village drinking to the failure of the Dance of the World. Two characters in *The Sailors Arms* are picked out for special attention.
The song sung by Mr Waldo is in quatrains ending in a six-line stanza.

Page 83, *Freudian reference:*

       O nobody's swept my chimbley
       Since my husband went his ways ...

and   Come and sweep my chimbley
       She sighed to me with a blush ...

During the final three pages the Second Voice appears only once again. The First Voice brings back Captain Cat three pages from the end: is this a deliberate effect of symmetry, since Captain Cat first appeared on page 3? Along with Captain Cat appear Rosie Probert, Dancing Williams, Jonah Jarvis, Organ Morgan, Cherry Owen (now drunk), Myfanwy

Price and Mog Edwards, and Mr Waldo rambling drunk through the wood. Polly Garter sings a snatch of her song, and the First Voice ends the play with an evocation of Llaregyb in the dark, windy night.

Page 86. Note *alliteration* and *consonantal pattern*. '... **the suddenly wind-shaken wood springs awake for the second dark time this one Spring day**' (*s - w, sh - w, s - w, s - d s - d*; wind-wood-wake-one).

It has already been suggested that *Under Milk Wood* falls naturally into four 'Acts' of equal length; another division would be into three 'Acts' corresponding to morning, noon and night. The play ends with this cycle beginning all over again, which is reminiscent of some lines of Dylan Thomas in his *Twenty Five Poems*

> Black night still ministers the moon,
> And the sky lays down her laws,
> The sea speaks in a kingly voice,
> Light and dark are no enemies
> But one companion.

12 The characters (a brief summary)

We are not wholly bad or good. ...

In *The Modern Age* (Pelican Guide to English Literature, 7, essay on 'T. F. Powys and Dylan Thomas') Holbrook writes, 'Thomas's lack of compassion culminates in the dramatic piece *Under Milk Wood* which, in that it is anything more than a commonplace piece of radio comedy, exhibits villagers in the spirit of malicious fun; two characters are described characteristically as "two old kippers in a box", Llaregyb is described as "a place of love": yet the only love in it is the sexual union of the drunken Mr Waldo and the promiscuous Polly Garter, offered for our approval. "We're all mad and nasty", but some are nastier than others, and our laughter at the goings-on at Llaregyb is a cruel laughter ... beneath the surface, Thomas hints, with a naughty leer and some crude gestures towards Freud (as, for example, with Mrs Willy Nilly), you will find people's impulses governed by childhood sins, and you will find dirty dreams and dirty desires. There is nothing essentially dramatic about the work, because the embodiments have no moral existence, and there is no conflict, development or synthesis: everything is of equally amusing interest, as to a child' (p. 417).

It is difficult to subscribe completely to this criticism: there is plenty of fun, but it is not all 'malicious'. Caitlin Thomas says that Dylan 'retained surprising loyalties to old buddies', but admits that one of their favourite kill-times in Laugharne was to sit in the window of Brown's Hotel and imagine the 'motherly bodies overlapping and spilling with fistfuls of fat' walking 'ten abreast up the street, stark naked' (*Leftover Life to Kill*, p. 36). Is there any malice in this? Malice means enmity of heart and ill will, and there seems to be little or none of this in *Under Milk Wood*.

It is true that most of the characters are unpleasant, un-savoury or psychologically abnormal people, but surely it is wrong to say that they are maliciously presented. 'There's a nasty lot live here when you come to think' (p. 46). Dylan Thomas seems to be saying, 'I want to show you a cross-section of life during a day in a village, to show you the people as they are, during a typical day. Most of the characters are thwarted, unhappy or unsavoury, but that is the way things are.' As the Reverend Eli Jenkins says,

> We are not wholly bad or good
> Who live our lives under Milk Wood,
> And thou, I know, will be the first,
> To see our best side, not our worst.

This seems to be the poet speaking: he shows us drunks, prostitutes, money-lovers (Mog Edwards 'hugs his lovely money to his own heart'), people living nostalgically in the past, religious hypocrites, gossips, and so one, but refrains from comment, except perhaps through the words of the Reverend Eli Jenkins.

Here follows a brief description of the female and male characters, and then, in the next Section, five of the characters are chosen for more detailed analysis.

Female characters	Brief description or pointer
Rosie Probert	*Fille de joie*, a '*good* bad girl'.
Waldo's mother	Presented in a favourable light?
Waldo's wife	Neurotic, terrified of what the neighbours will say.
The Four Neighbours	Narrow-minded gossips.
Matti's mother	'Screaming' (p. 12).

The Five Women	No indication given, apart, perhaps from their names.
Mrs Ogmore-Pritchard	'Husband-killer' – cleanliness is next to godliness.
Gossamer Beynon	Dreams of 'a small rough ready man with a bush tail'. Wants to be 'refined'.
Mrs Floyd	Physical unattractiveness of old age – toothless – 'old kipper'.
Mrs Utah Watkins	Bleats like a sheep.
Mrs Willy Nilly	'Whimpers' – 'every night of her married life she has been late for school'; 'double-chinned'.
Mae Rose Cottage	Wishful thinker – 'call me Dolores as they do in the stories'. Frustrated adolescent.
Bessie Bighead	Physically unattractive – 'smelling of the cowshed, snores bass and gruff'.
Mrs Organ Morgan	Looks 'dead beat'; with her husband it's 'organ organ all the time'.
Mary Ann Sailors	'Dreams of the Garden of Eden'.
Polly Garter	Dreams of babies; indifferent to her reputation.
Lily Smalls	One of the few normal, balanced characters, but a 'baggage'.
Mrs Pugh	Frigid and fussy; husband entertains thoughts of poisoning her.
Mrs Beynon	Domineering, likes to be waited on – 'Where's my tea, girl?'
Mrs Dai Bread One	Likes to take it easy. Physical comfort is the most important thing in life – 'nice to be comfy, nice to be nice'.
Mrs Dai Bread Two	Conscious of her animal attractions.
Miss Price	Spinster of precise habits – 'natty as a jenny-wren, then pit-pat back to my egg in its cosy . . .'.
Mrs Cherry Owen	Her husband can do no wrong – she laughs 'delightedly' at his drunken antics. Mother-complex – 'And then I got you into bed'.

Male characters	**Brief description or pointer**
Captain Cat	Lives in the past – 'Oh, my dead dears!'
Mr Edwards	'A draper mad with love', but a man who 'hugs his lovely money to his *own* heart'.
Mr Waldo	'There's a husband for you' – 'Bad as his father' – 'What he'll do for drink'.
Mr Willy Nilly	The name is significant (*having no regard for one's wishes*) – 'Rat-a-tats hard and sharp on Mrs Willy Nilly'.

Sinbad Sailors	Unrequited love – 'hugs his damp pillow whose secret name is Gossamer Beynon'.
Mr Pugh	Murderous intent.
Dai Bread	'Dreams of harems.'
Lord Cut-Glass	Eccentric.
Cherry Owen	Irresponsible drunkard.
Butcher Beynon	'He's the biggest liar in town.'
Nogood Boyo	Irreligious – 'I don't know who's up there and I don't care'.
Jack Black	Spies on courting couples.

13 A more detailed consideration of five characters

i) *Captain Cat*
Oh, my dead dears!

In the poet's talk *Quite Early One Morning*, broadcast in 1945, the essential germ of *Under Milk Wood* is discernible:

> I am Captain Tiny Evans, my ship was the Kidwelly.
> And Mrs Tiny Evans has been dead for many a year.

Captain Cat first appears at the end of the opening speech of the First Voice (p. 3) and is described as a 'retired blind sea-captain'. He lives in Schooner House, in which, apparently, a nautical atmosphere has been created.

Page 3. *Alliteration* Seashelled, ship-in-bottled, shipshape, help to produce an effect of swishing water.
Internal rhyme **Sea, asleep, sea, dreams, seas, deep;** and **seashelled, Kidwelly, bellying**.
nibble Used also in the poem 'I in My Intricate Image' (*Collected Poems*, p. 37).
Kidwell Municipal borough near the mouth of the river Gwendraeth, on Carmarthen Bay, with a fine castle.
Nantucket A small North American island off the coast of Massachusetts, once an important whaling-station.

Captain Cat next appears in his galley where he, 'blind and fine-fingered, savours his fish-fry'.

Page 32. Note *alliteration* **Fine-fingered, sea-fry**; also *internal rhyme*: **blind, fine-fingered, fry**. *Example of cynghanedd*: **savours his sea-fry** $(s - v - r, s - f - r)$.

A little later Captain Cat hears the school-bell in the back-ground (p. 38), and repeats to himself the names of some of the children going to school. Maggie Richards, Ricky Rhys,

Tommy Powell. . . . He then (p. 38) hears the postman knock-
ing at the door of Mrs Ogmore-Pritchard's house, Bay View.

Page 39, *alliteration* Repetition of s-sounds to produce a slippery
  effect: swabs, glassy, soap, size, twelveses, Bessie, beeswax, birds,
  slip.
Page 40, **polish the potatoes** Although Dylan Thomas did not
  do any military service, this is probably an allusion to the former
  practice in some army-camps of making a fetish of excessive
  cleanliness, e.g. whitewashing the coke.

Captain Cat, though blind, can recognize the village people
from their walk or voices. There has already been one example
of this on page 38 ('Billy Swansea with the dog's voice'). He
now hears the tread of the postman, Willy Nilly, whose feet
are 'heavy on the distant cobbles'. By counting the postman's
steps, he knows that the latter has stopped at the house of Mrs
Rose Cottage, then at School House and Manchester House.
Captain Cat knows everything that is going on in the village
('Today she gets the letter from her sister in Gorslas', and
'blind Captain Cat hears all the morning of the town' (p. 38).
At the sound of quicker feet approaching, Captain Cat recognizes Mr Waldo hurrying to *The Sailors Arms* (p. 41); since the
footsteps stop, however, Captain Cat knows that the postman
is handing a letter to Mr Waldo.

Captain Cat now makes his first long speech (p. 42). This
speech has a useful function in that it introduces movement
into the play and gives a cross-section of village life. Captain
Cat recognizes numerous female characters from the sound
they make when they walk: Mrs Cherry, who trots; Mrs Dai
Bread One, 'waltzing up the street like a jelly'; Mae, the eldest
daughter of Mrs Rose Cottage, already wearing high heels.
There is also a group of women chattering round the pump;
Ocky Milkman on his round. The sudden hush round the
pump indicates to Captain Cat that Polly Garter is coming.

Page 43, **gandering hubbies** Word-play on 'wandering', i.e.
  sexually errant husbands. A gander is a male goose.

At the end of the morning (p. 56) Captain Cat is still sitting
at his window listening to the village sounds.

He does not appear again until the afternoon (p. 68), when
the First Voice shows him taking a nap at his open window,
weeping in his sleep at his memories.

The student should compare the speech of First Voice

(p. 68) with the first stanza of 'Light Breaks Where no Sun
Shines' (*Collected Poems*, p. 34):

> Light breaks where no sun shines;
> Where no sea runs; the waters of the heart
> Push in their tides;
> And, broken ghosts with glow-warms in their heads,
> The things of light
> File through the flesh where no flesh decks the bones.

Page 68, *alliteration* **Sun – seas – sailed – slumbers; belly –
brawls – broken – bottles – babel – bars.**
Internal rhyme **Cows – souses – blowzy; weeps – sleeps,
clippered sea,** sea full of sailing clippers.
Page 68, *cynghanedd* **Haven – heaven** (*h - v - n, h - v - n*).

In his sleep, Rosie Probert is speaking, addressing him as
Tom Cat, and referring to him as her master and bosun, an
allusion to his former sexual vigour. Here again there is much
musical repetition of certain vowel sounds:

Page 69, *internal rhyme* **Sea – beasts – green; seas – seals –
green – eels.**
Page 70, *internal rhyme* **Easy – sweetheart – seas – bean – seal.**
seal-barking moon A favourite device of Dylan Thomas, cf. 'pig-
loving sun' (p. 67).

Captain Cat reveals that whilst at sea his thoughts were full
of Rosie Probert:

> The only sea I saw
> Was the seesaw sea
> With you riding upon it.

This is an oblique allusion to love-making, as is shown in
the next two lines:

> Lie down, lie easy
> Let me shipwreck in your thighs.

At this memory Captain Cat weeps. He is last seen at dusk,
climbing into his bunk (p. 84) and thinking of acquaintances
in his past life.
The next lines beginning '*Remember her*' are regarded by
Holbrook as Dylan Thomas's 'most serious lines' which,
however, 'reveal how pathetically short Thomas falls of any-

thing approaching real drama'. Dylan Thomas, says Holbrook, regards as important the relationship between Captain Cat and Rosie Probert, whom he shared with Tom, Fred the Donkeyman and other sailors. 'What do Rosie's lines mean, beyond a gesture at feelings appropriate to dead people? If she is dead, how can she be "forgetting"? This is a dream of her, of course: but the lines take on a serious modulation (the rhythm having gone significantly flat) and we expect a general statement about Death. "The earth which filled her mouth Is vanishing from her". What can this mean? "Getting a mouthful of mould" is a country expression, dry, ironical, stoical, for dying. But how "vanishing from her"?' Holbrook points out that the origin of 'I am going into the darkness of the darkness for ever' is T. S. Eliot's, 'They all go into the dark ...' (*Difficulties of a Statesman*). Holbrook then compares unfavourably the 'nibbling fishes' with an extract from James Joyce's *Ulysses*. Thomas's writing is described as 'playful immaturity', that of Joyce as 'organized vitality'. In the case of Joyce 'the writing moves, controlled, towards a philosophic contemplation of the tragic nature of life' (see *Llareggub Revisited*, pp. 210–12).

It seems reasonable to suppose that Captain Cat is based upon a real figure, an ancient mariner actually known to Dylan Thomas. He is a man who has long lived in retirement in the village and knows everyone in it. He becomes very sentimental over his memories, but at the same time has a wry sense of humour:

> 'Ocky Milkman on his round. I will say this, his milk's
> as fresh as the dew. Half dew it is'.

(The Section on Captain Cat speaking the dreams that take him back to a life at sea was apparently one of the first 'fragments' to be written by Dylan Thomas – fragments that were to be later 'expanded' into *Under Milk Wood*.)

ii) *The Reverend Eli Jenkins*
Praise the Lord! We are a musical nation.
The Reverend Eli Jenkins is, with Captain Cat, one of the two 'moral centres' of the play: 'the Reverend with his touching "good-bad" poems and his appeals to a gentle God to look forgivingly on human weaknesses; and Captain Cat, whose fire of lust and love ... is not quenched even by the waters of

death and of utter forgiveness. Thomas was, as a man, like the Reverend Eli Jenkins, utterly without malice' (Fraser).

The first mention of the Reverend Eli Jenkins is on page 20, where he is introduced by First Voice as a poet and preacher, turning in his 'deep, towards-dawn sleep' and dreaming of 'Eisteddfodau'. He is introduced again, this time by Second Voice (p. 24) in a manner that is 'sympathetic and right, a caricature, but Dickensian and sympathetic' (Holbrook).

Page 20, **Eisteddfod** (plural *Eisteddfodau*) is a Bardic congress held periodically in Wales for the encouragement and development of Welsh poetry and music. Its origins go back to pre-Christian times, but the first recorded *Eisteddfod* was held in the 6th century.

crwth A stringed instrument.

pibgorn A wind instrument.

druid A member of a religious order in ancient Gaul, Britain and Ireland. The chief prehistoric monument of druidism in Britain is Stonehenge, a circular group of large stones on Salisbury Plain, belonging to the Neolithic or Bronze Age. The word is also used in 'Poem on His Birthday' (*Collected Poems*, p. 172) — 'druid heron vows'.

parch preacher (Welsh).

The Reverend Eli Jenkins first appears in the early morning (p. 24). He is the village parson and bard who lives in Bethesda House. His first act after dressing is to stand at the front door of his house, look up at the 'eternal hill' (Llaregyb Hill) and listen to the sounds of the morning. His 'morning service' consists in the recitation of one of his own poems; it is aparently a daily act, since later (p. 28) Mrs Pugh asks, 'Has Mr Jenkins said his poetry?'.

The play contains two poems read by the Reverend Eli Jenkins (pp. 24–5 and p. 79). The first poem is regarded by Holbrook as a 'good pastiche', which 'lightly satirizes and exactly catches the style of local newspaper verse'. In its general impact, it is true, the poem hardly rises above this level, but there are skilful lines which are typical of the poet, and which would hardly be found in amateur verse, e.g. ll.3–4, stanza 1, '*fairer hills and loftier far, And grows more full of flowers*' (f-r, f-r, f-r); and last line, penultimate stanza: '*Love all my life and longer*' (l-v-l, l-f-l). Several of the stanzas evince an obvious delight in the sound of Welsh topographical names.

Stanzas 3 and 4 include several names of mountains, contrasted with the size and grandeur of which tiny Llaregyb Hill is only a 'molehill':

Page 24. **Cader Idris** A mountain in North Wales to the east of Barmouth (2,927 feet).

Moel yr Wyddfa Mount Snowdon (3,560 feet).

Carnedd Llewellyn Another mountain in North Wales, to the south-east of Bethesda (3,485 feet).

Plinlimmon (alternative spelling Plynlimmon). A mountain in central Wales, to the east of Aberystwyth (2,468 feet).

Page 25 **Penmaenmawr** (=big, black rock). A mountainous promontory in North Wales near the town of that name, facing Conway Bay.

Stanzas 5 and 6 contain the names of rivers of which the most important, Dovey, Dee, Taff, Towy, Cleddau will be found on an ordinary atlas map.

King of time A geological formation of great age.

(The rhyme-scheme throughout is *a - b - a - b*, with the exception of stanza 7, which is *a - b - c - b*.)

The Reverend Eli Jenkins next appears on page 32, where, already at breakfast time, he is busy composing verses. He does not re-appear until the late morning (p. 54), when he is visiting the sick 'with jelly and poems', after praising the Lord that the Welsh are a musical nation.

In addition to his poems the Reverend Eli is at work on a prose-work ('his Lifework') dealing with the history and natural history of Llaregyb, called 'the White Book of Llaregyb'.

Page 74, **white book** Strictly speaking, an official report of Government affairs (e.g. Germany, Portugal); in England the term *White Paper* is used. Vernon Watkins (in *Letters to Dylan Thomas*) informs us that at one time 'white' was a favourite adjective of Dylan Thomas. The word 'white', apart from its use as an adjective of colour, also means 'without evil intent; relatively harmless'. (See also note on p. 5.)

Just as the Reverend Eli Jenkins greets each new day with a poem, so does he recite a poem at sunset (p. 79). This poem of four stanzas is oddly reminiscent of the hymn,

New every morning is Thy love,
Our waking and uprising prove.
Through sleep and darkness safely brought,
Restored to life and power and thought.

There is also an echo of Dylan Thomas's poem 'When I Woke' (*Collected Poems*, p. 134):

> 'Every morning I make
> God in bed, good or bad'.

The rhyme-scheme is *a - a - b - b* throughout. In its simplicity this little poem shows the influence of A. E. Housman.

We next hear of the Reverend Eli Jenkins when, once more in his parlour or 'poem-room', he is at work on his 'White Book' (p. 82).

Page 82, **tumulus** a hillock or sepulchral mound; ancient grave or 'barrow'.

peoples that dwelt ... This is a reference to the first inhabitants of Wales, small dark people (known in Welsh as *pobl fach*), who probably came from north Africa through Spain and France. They were the cromlech-builders, people speaking a language perhaps related to Berber, the modern language spoken in North Africa, or even to Basque. This physical type is still occasionally seen in the population of Wales, as was pointed out in an article by Professor H. J. Fleure many years ago in the *Manchester Guardian* – 'Geography in the Blood' (see also E. J. Bowen: *Wales*). Dylan Thomas himself belonged physically to the *pobl fach*.

the Celts The term *Celtic* is a misleading one, and should strictly be reserved for the group of languages (Welsh, Irish, Gaelic, Manx, Cornish, Breton). In its original form, *Keltoi*, as used by the Greeks, the term was applied to all fair-haired, blue-eyed and tall people living north of the Alps. The original home of the Celts, as deduced from linguistic evidence, was in South-west Germany, near the head-waters of the Danube (see Elston, *The Earliest Contacts of Germans and Celts*). The religion of the French (Gallic) and British Celts before Romanization was *druidism*.

the Land of Summer May refer to the original home of the Celts mentioned above. It may have been stimultaneously intended as a play on the name *Sumer*, the early civilization of the plain of Shinar (later Babylonia) to indicate a remote origin.

The Reverend Eli Jenkins is fittingly the last person to appear in the play, and reveals his essentially pantheistic attitude, viewing Milk Wood as 'a greenleaved sermon on the innocence of men'.

It is interesting to observe that there is a possible forerunner of the Reverend Eli Jenkins, with the same druidic leanings, in

Dylan Thomas's story. 'The Enemies' (first published in *New Stories*, 1934), reproduced in *A Prospect of the Sea*): 'loving his God, he had loved the darkness where men of old had worshipped the dark invisible'.

iii) *Mrs Ogmore-Pritchard*
And before you let the sun in, mind it wipes its shoes.

Mrs Ogmore-Pritchard is introduced by the First Voice. She has been twice widowed; her first husband was Mr Ogmore, a retired keeper of a linoleum-shop; her second husband was Mr Pritchard, a 'failed bookmaker'. The First Voice presents Mrs Ogmore-Pritchard in the light of a very fussy, house-proud woman. It seems legitimate to read into Dylan Thomas's choice of language a sexually frigid woman who has dominated and 'organized' the lives of both her former husbands.

We see her first 'in her iceberg-white, holily laundered crinoline nightgown, under virtuous polar sheets, in her spruced and scoured dust-defying bedroom', phrases reminiscent of the 'antiseptic sheets' of another well-known Welsh writer, Rhys Davies, in his novel *The Red Hills*. She lives at the top of the town, keeping a house (Bay View) for paying guests.

Page 14. Note *vowel patternization* **in her iceberg-white, holily laundered crinoline nightgown**; notice also the interesting short and long *i*-sounds: ice – white – night; in – holily – crinoline, night-gown.

trig and trim Bay View A tautologous expression – *trig* also means 'trim', 'smart', 'spruce' (which occurs in the previous phrase).

alliteration This passage (First Voice) is highly alliterative:
– dust-defying
– trig and trim
– fume of polish, ironically-swallowed disinfectant, fidgets. . . .

failed bookmaker Might have been suggested to Dylan Thomas by the expression, common in India, 'failed B.A.'.

besoming From 'besom', a broom made of sticks. There appears to be word-play here, i.e. 'bosoming': Mr Pritchard is maddened by the interfering female, who not only gives him these tedious tasks to perform but also constantly watches him to see that he does them to her satisfaction.

fume Strictly speaking, *fume* refers to a smoke or vapour but, since floor polish impregnates the atmosphere and seems to hang in it like smoke, it is a happy choice here.

rinsed sleep This phrase is all of a piece with two earlier ones, *holily laundered* and *virtuous polar sheets*. *Rinse* comes from

French *rincer*, which perhaps in turn came from medieval Latin *re sincerare*, from *sincerus*, 'pure'.

Pages 14–16. Examples of Mrs Ogmore-Pritchard's domineering ways with her husbands. In her dream she tells their ghosts to repeat the 'Tasks' she has set them:

Mr Ogmore
Inhale balsam.
Put pyjamas in drawer marked pyjamas.
Wear a flannel band to ward off sciatica.
Blow his nose in a piece of tissue which he must afterwards burn.
Boil the drinking-water because of germs.
Have a charcoal biscuit, which is good for him.
Put on rubber gloves and search the 'peke' (pekinese dog) for fleas.

Mr Pritchard
Inhale balsam.
Take a cold bath, which is 'good' for him.
Dress behind the curtain and put on his apron.
Take his salts, 'which are nature's friend'.
Make his herb-tea, which is 'free from tannin'.
Smoke one pipe of asthma-mixture. (But only in the woodshed.)
Dust the parlour and spray the canary.
Dust the blinds and then raise them. (Then comes the delightful phrase, 'And before you let the sun in, mind it wipes its shoes'.)

It should be noted that Mrs Ogmore-Pritchard appears also in *Quite Early One Morning*:

'Open the curtains, light the fire, what are servants for?
I am Mrs Ogmore-Pritchard and I want another snooze.
Dust the china, feed the canary, sweep the drawing-room floor;
And before you let the sun in, mind he wipes his shoes.'

The next appearance of Mrs Ogmore-Pritchard is when Willy Nilly the postman brings her a letter (p. 39) from an ornithologist who requires accommodation for two weeks.

Page 39, **Builth Wells** An urban district parish and town of Breconshire, Wales, a noted salmon-fishing centre.

The last part of Willy Nilly's speech is elliptical, i.e. *bath* is understood to be followed by a hyphen and '*he is a vegetarian*'. Once again we are given an example of Mrs Ogmore-Pritchard's mania for cleanliness and tidiness. She is afraid that her 'nice clean rooms' will be made untidy by the birdwatcher 'covered with feathers', 'breathing all over the chairs', 'putting (his) feet on my carpets and sneezing on my china and sleeping in my sheets'. Captain Cat terminates this little scene by saying, 'And back she goes to the kitchen to polish the potatoes', once again pointing to Mrs Ogmore-Pritchard's obsessional concern with cleanliness, which in turn is related to chapel-teaching ('Cleanliness is next to godliness'). David Holbrook believes that Dylan Thomas here 'sets out to expose the hatred of life expressed in the neat suburban home ... the deathly hygienic denial of Mrs Ogmore-Pritchard is but the obverse of his own shrinking from the actualities of physical sex ...' (*Llareggub Revisited*, p. 231).

Mrs Ogmore-Pritchard again appears at dusk (p. 76), and again Dylan Thomas uses the First Voice to evoke a picture of a prim, desiccated, brittle woman.

'Mrs Ogmore-Pritchard at the first drop of the dusk-shower, seals all her sea-view doors, draws the germ-free blinds, sits, erect as a dry dream on a high-backed hygienic chair and wills herself to cold, quick sleep'; whereupon the ghosts of her two husbands reappear.

Alliteration. There is careful alliteration (seals − sea − sits; dry dream, dead day, sigh and sidle); and vowel-repetition (high − hygienic) as in the speech of the First Voice (p. 14). The vowel patternization is very elaborate, as the student will perceive if he writes out the vowel sounds only of this speech.

acid love *Acid* as an adjective means 'sour'; the phrase is evocative of *acid test* (acid is used to test chemical composition) which can be used figuratively to relate to morals. 'There is acid love in her voice for one of the two shambling phantoms.'

tears where their eyes once were Evocative of Shakespeare's *The Tempest.*

The final speech of this scene (p. 78) parallels the speech in the opening scene (p. 14) of the Ogmore-Pritchard sequence:

Page 14	Page 78
Soon it will be time to get up.	Soon it will be time to go to bed.
Tell me your tasks, in order.	Tell me your tasks in order.

The cycle is thus complete. We first meet Mrs Ogmore-Pritchard as she 'fidgets in her sleep', then in the morning as the postman brings her the letter. The last time we see her, at dusk, she has fallen asleep in her high-backed chair.

Dylan Thomas thus gives us a very vivid cameo of a certain type of shrill virago who is a common type in Welsh villages, an ascetic, sexually frigid termagant who wears a *crinoline* nightdress. The use of this word (which originally referred to a stiff cloth made of horse-hair and linen thread) creates the atmosphere for the subsequent impressions. Her dual passions are cleanliness and order; she sees death lurking in every corner of the house, and even the canary has to sprayed. (What Dylan Thomas probably had in mind here was the disease known as *psittacosis*, a contagious disease, especially of parrots, which can be communicated to man in the form of bronchial fever, nausea, even pneumonia.)

The relatively large part of *Under Milk Wood* devoted to Mrs Ogmore-Pritchard, and the light in which is presented by Dylan Thomas are indicative of his preoccupation with the borderlands of sexual experience and religion, especially the religious doctrines and practices of the Welsh chapel.

iv) *Polly Garter*
Oh, isn't life a terrible thing, thank God?

Henry Treece (in *Dylan Thomas: Dog Among the Fairies*, p. 143) refers to Polly Garter as 'the good-natured loose woman of the place, . . . the easy consort of any man', who is 'both the warm Goddess of Fertility, the life-giver to so many, but also the fleshly memory of many who are now dead. They live on only in her song, which, in Daniel Jones's plaintive and rather acidic settings, assaults the heart again and again, as it should be assaulted, without sentimentality, the wistful melody underpinning the poet's reminder of our immutable destiny.'

She is first introduced at the end of 'Act I' (p. 22), dreaming of babies and, a little later, Mrs Pugh says that P.C. Attila Rees is going to arrest Polly 'for having babies' (p. 28). She is thus presented immediately as the *fille de joie* of the town, with a numerous progeny begotten by unknown fathers: 'Nothing grows in our garden, only washing. And babies. And where's their fathers live, my love? Over the hills and far away' (p. 30). She accepts her fate quite calmly, however, even gladly: 'Oh, isn't life a terrible thing, thank God?' (p. 31).

David Holbrook (*Llareggub Revisited*, pp. 230–1), regards Polly Garter's conversation with her baby (pp. 30–1) as 'a plea for an impossible infantile moral anarchy – there is no suffering here because the child does not know which is its father, of Polly's many violators'. He believes that the desire of

Dylan Thomas was 'to convince us that in this amoral world there is no suffering, as a conseqence of the kind of "love" he himself is forced by his sickness to seek – that is, the satisfaction of sexual needs without the acceptance of responsibility. . . . The sentimentality lies in the utter impossibility of such a complacent speech, in any real sense, from such a woman who in reality would suffer in many ways from her weaknesses, and deserve our pity'. There is some force in this criticism, but whether such complacency is impossible is to be doubted. Certainly Polly Garter seems to have no visible means of support. Her goings-on form the stock-in-trade of the women's gossip round the pump ('seen Polly Garter giving her belly an airing'), and Captain Cat (p. 43) knows by the sudden hush round the pump that Polly is approaching. Dylan Thomas's reference to the Mothers' Union Social Dance as 'that wedding-ringed holy' shows where his sympathy lies.

Polly Garter's long song (p. 54) consists of rhyming couplets. There is also a snatch of song on p. 56, where the word 'loving' is substituted by 'ding-a-ding', and at the end of the play (p. 86). Little Willie Wee is regarded by Holbrook as the child-Thomas himself, but there seems to be no real evidence for this.* It should be noted, however, that at the end of the song 'Wee' becomes 'Weazel', i.e. *weasel*. According to Partridge (*Dictionary of Slang*) the word is partly of erotic origin: Little Willie Weazel would then refer to a sexually active little man.

v) *Mae Rose Cottage*
I'll sin till I blow up!

'Dylan Thomas knew the appeal of the salacious. He renders a drunk dream, or an erotic dream, under no control but that of verbal pyrotechnics, with naughty hints, for its own sake' (D. Holbrook). This is undoubtedly true, but it is found in many other writers. Much as the present writer has gained from Holbrook's study, he agrees with a recent reviewer in *The Listener* that there is a 'nagging tone and fanatical moralizing' in it. (*Llareggub Revisited* is, however, 'for all its evangelistic rigour and unpleasantness of talk, at least an attempt at true criticism'.)

---

* It is interesting to note not only that is there a character named Polly in Dylan Thomas's *Adventures in the Skin Trade* (1955) but also that she expressed the same sentiments as Polly Garter: ' "His name was Sam and he had green eyes and brown hair. He was ever so short. Darling, darling, darling Sam, he's dead." The tears ran down her cheeks' (p. 76).

Mae Rose Cottage, seventeen years old, first appears in 'Act I' (p. 19) when the Second Voice introduces her as Mrs Rose Cottage's eldest daughter. The language which follows – 'in a furnace in a tower in a cave in a waterfall in a wood' – is reminiscent of a compound Welsh placename. Mae is presented as a repressed adolescent identifying herself with 'romantic' heroines ('Call me Dolores/Like they do in the stories') and waiting for the right man to come along.

She is not heard again until 'Act IV' (p. 73), where she is drowsing in the field of nannygoats.

Page 73, **puffball** Any of various fungi which discharge the ripe spores when struck or blown.
Alliteration Lazily she lies alone. . . .

Later, as dusk is falling (p. 78) we see her still lying in the clover; 'she listens to the nannygoats chew, draws circles of lipstick round her nipples' (compare Gossamer Beynon's '*red*-berried breast' – p. 60, and Mr Waldo smacking 'his live *red* lips' – p. 85). She realizes her physical need and knows that she would be considered wicked in the eyes of the chapel-goers:

> I'm fast. I'm a bad lot. God will strike me dead.
> I'm seventeen. I'll go to hell,

she says to the goats.

The purpose of this character seems to be to show the struggle – a struggle easily abandoned – of the stirrings of adolescence with the social code which such a community tries to impose. It is perhaps significant that when we leave Mae 'waiting for the worst to happen' we immediately hear the Reverend Eli Jenkins reciting his sunset poem, in which he tells us that: 'We are not wholly good or bad'. This seems to be the attitude of the poet himself: throughout this play the characters are allowed mainly to speak for themselves, without any commentary, favourable or unfavourable, which might have been given through the First or Second Voices. Perhaps Dylan Thomas expresses himself through Jonah Jarvis – 'come to a bad end, very enjoyable' (p. 4).

14 The physical presence of the village
A backwater of life

The play *Under Milk Wood*, as G. S. Fraser has pointed out, does not derive from any literary model, but from the radio 'feature' form, 'in narrative and dialogue, evoking the spirit of a place'.

The most substantial description of the setting is that given by the Voice of a Guide Book, which occurs, appropriately, at the beginning of 'Act II', at sunrise, when 'the town ripples like a lake in the waking haze' (p. 22). It is now becoming light, and the small town can be seen.

It is a village of 'less than five hundred souls' – 'a small, decaying watering-place', boasting three main streets, some narrow by-lanes and scattered farmsteads. This section (p. 23) is an admirable imitation of the flat, objective approach of the typical guide-book.

The main street is Coronation Street, consisting mostly of 'humble, two-storied houses', and a few more pretentious but dilapidated eighteenth-century houses. It is, however, a picturesque, even 'quaint' place with 'its cobbled streets and its little fishing-harbour, its several curious customs'. The river Dewi flows through the village; it is mentioned again in Stanza 6 of the Reverend Eli Jenkins's poem (p. 25). The small town is dominated by the 'mystic tumulus' of Llaregyb Hill, and is irregularly disposed: thus we read (p. 85) of the 'top' of the town and the 'sea end'. The flank of Llaregyb Hill is clothed with the wood that gives the play its title: 'the hunched, courters'-and-rabbits' wood limping invisible down to the sloeblack, slow, black, crowblack, fishingboat-bobbing sea'.

Three of the streets are named: Coronation Street, Cockle Row and Donkey Street. The latter name may be based on the name Cwmdonkin Park in Swansea or, more probably, it may refer to the street on which cocklewomen formerly rode their donkeys. There is 'one place of worship, and one public-house, *The Sailors Arms*'.

The pervasive presence of the sea is felt throughout the play. In the first speeches of First and Second Voice, we hear of the 'webfoot cocklewomen', 'the jollyrodgered sea', 'the black, dab-filled sea', 'night ... trotting silent, with seaweed on its hooves', 'the slow deep salt and silent, black, bandaged night', and 'the seashelled, ship-in-bottled, shipshape best cabin of Schooner House'. The first character to be introduced is Captain Cat, dreaming of 'never such seas as any that swamped the decks of his S.S. *Kidwelly* bellying over the bedclothes and jellyfish-slippery sucking him down salt deep into the Davy dark ...'. Later in 'Act I' we hear of 'the dreamers in the streets rocked to sleep by the sea' and 'the wrecks and sprats and shells and fishbones, whalejuice and moonshine* and small salt fry dished up by the hidden sea'.

At the beginning of 'Act II' (p. 23) the Voice of a Guide Book refers to the 'small, decaying watering-place' and its inhabitants who possess 'a salty individuality of their own'. (There is, however, little opportunity for the poet to bring out this individuality, since the characters are too numerous and with one or two exceptions, are paste-board figures.) Llaregyb Hill is mentioned several times – on p. 22 by the First Voice, again on p. 23 by the First Voice ('our green hill'), in the Reverend Eli Jenkins's poem (p. 25), by the First Voice again on p. 37 and p. 47, and by Mary Ann Sailors on p. 48, and the play ends (p. 86) with a reference to 'Llaregyb's land'.

There is again a salty tang about 'Act II': on p. 36 the First Voice refers to the 'cockled cobbles' and, a little later, the Second Voice continues with references to the fishermen, and the 'dab-filled bay'. At the commencement of 'Act III' (p. 44) the estuary and the sea figure again in the long speech of the First Voice: 'the gulls' gab and rabble on the boat-bobbing river and sea and the cockles bubbling in the sand . . .'. Shrimp-nets are sold in Mrs Organ Morgan's general shop. The speech of the First Voice on p. 47 gives us an excellent impression of a fine spring morning with a tangy breeze blowing through the town; 'Spring whips green down Cockle Row, and the shells ring out. Llaregyb this snip of a morning is wild-fruit and warm, the streets, fields, sands and waters springing in the young sun.'

A sea-view is provided again by the Second Voice on p. 50: 'herring gulls heckling down to the harbour where the fishermen spit and prop the morning up and eye the fishy sea smooth to the sea's end as it lulls in blue'. In the final 'Act', Nogood Boyo is seen fishing in 'the still middle of the blue-bagged bay' (p. 72).

On p. 74 we hear that not only is the Reverend Eli Jenkins the local bard, but also the chronicler and topographer of the town. His 'Lifework' dealing with 'the Population, Main Industry, Shipping, History, Topography, Flora and Fauna' is being written in the White Book of Llaregyb. (The so-called Four Ancient Books of Wales, first edited by W. F. Skene, Edinburgh, 1868, are: *The Black Book of Carmarthen*, late 12th

---

* Illicitly distilled liquor, especially whisky.

century; *The Book of Aneirin*, about 1250; *The Book of Taliesin*, about 1275; and *The Red Book of Hergest*, about 1400. Other important manuscripts are *The White Book of Rhydderch*; *The White Book of Mabinogion*; *The Red Book of Talgarth*.)

At nightfall (p. 81) the sea again makes its presence felt, and the First Voice refers to the 'larrupped waves' (from 'larrup', 'flog or beat soundly', i.e. waves lashed by the wind).

It is thus possible to reconstruct the physical setting of the play. The picture of the town is made more vivid by reference to several tradesmen and their activities: the baker, Dai Bread; the milkman, Ocky Milkman; the dressmaker and sweetshop-keeper, Miss Price; the draper, Mr Mog Edwards; the undertaker, Evans the Death; the jack-of-all trades, Mister Waldo ('rabbitcatcher, barber, herbalist, catdoctor, quack'); the butcher, Beynon; the organist, Organ Morgan; the cocklers, Mr and Mrs Floyd; the policeman, P.C. Attila Rees; the poet and preacher, the Reverend Eli Jenkins; the housemaid, Lily Smalls; the schoolmaster, Mr Pugh; the groceress, Mrs Organ Morgan; the postman, Willy Nilly; the schoolmistress, Gossamer Beynon; some of the communal activities of the town are mentioned, e.g. the glee-singers (p. 51) and the Mothers' Union Dance (p. 53), the fishermen who, at the slightest excuse, go drinking in *The Sailors Arms*. We hear of the town's unmarried girls (p. 81) and the wolf-whistles of the young men (p. 82). The movement is further enlivened by the children's play (pp. 56–9).

The poet was thus at pains to produce a realistic setting and a tangible atmosphere for his play. It would be wrong to equate Llaregyb with Laugharne, but it is reasonable to assume that Laugharne and other parts of the South Wales coast were present in his mind when he was writing this play.

Note on cockling: The chief Welsh area for cockle-gathering is Carmarthen Bay, the beds stretching from Laugharne, through Ferryside and Pwll to Whitford Point. The cockles are collected daily by women who ride on donkeys or in pony-carts (see M. E. Hughes and A. J. James: *Wales*, London, 1961, pp. 123–5).

15 Conclusion

In these *Notes* the student has been given ample suggestions and material for the study and appreciation of *Under Milk Wood*, and this final work has been linked up with aspects of Thomas's poetry and other prose-works. It is worth while

repeating that although Dylan Thomas was under considerable pressure to produce the final version, the actual gestation
had occupied him for no less than ten years, during which
time there must have been numerous versions of different
parts of the play, at least in the poet's head. How otherwise
can one account for the 'links', some of which have been
indicated in these Notes, between Under Milk Wood and
Thomas's other works?

Estimates of the value of Dylan Thomas's poetry and prose
will always vary greatly, at least until we have had time to see
him in proper perspective. Under Milk Wood cannot be regarded as a masterpiece, but it is at least a highly individual
and interesting example of a new genre. It is also a very
entertaining play and one evocative of the Welsh scene. It is
not for nothing that its author insisted that Welsh voices were
necessary for the first American production. In view of this
one should reconsider Holbrook's strictures that Llaregyb is
nothing more than a 'toy-town'. The play has its roots in
Laugharne and similar small towns in South Wales, and
many of its characters are recognizable Welsh types. The
author of these Notes lived for a year in a small Welsh village
and his dominant impression on a first reading of the play
was, 'I have been there before'.*

Immediately following this section is a list of General Questions which will enable the student to come to grips with the
play in its more detailed aspects. Remember that it was conceived as a 'radio play', a 'play for voices', and that therefore,
owing to the large number of characters, it was essential to
have some guiding thread running through the whole play to
prevent it from degeneration into utter amorphousness. The
First and Second Voices are the device adopted to give shape
and continuity, and they are successfully used. Although it is a
radio play, it was performed with success on the stage and
would undoubtedly lend itself for adaptation to television. It
would, indeed, be a good exercise for the student to attempt to
write down some directions for the producer of a television
play. The First and Second Voices would then be 'talking
cameras' directing our attention to the various scenes and
characters in the village. Run quickly through the play and
notice the stage-directions. The play opens with the direction

* Thomas himself called Under Milk Wood 'an impression for voices, an entertainment out of the darkness, of the town I live in' (quoted T. H. Jones: Dylan Thomas,
p. 91).

'Silence' and the First Voice then speaks 'very softly', because it is night and everything is still and quiet. There is no further stage-direction until p. 7 when we hear 'Noise of money-tills and chapel-bells'. What is the significance of this collocation of 'money-tills' and 'chapel-bells'? (see p. 85). Some of the stage-directions help to enforce the indications given by the First and Second Voices as to the passage of time, e.g. on p. 23 'A cock crows', and this is followed by the 'Slow bell notes' of the townhall bell, heard again after the Reverend Eli Jenkins has finished his morning prayer.

Under Milk Wood shows its author's gifts for humour and deft characterization, as well as his poetic gifts. It must be viewed as a culmination, in many ways, of his previous work and as a pointer to his development had he lived. It would be strange if the study of this work did not lead the reader to find out more about the author and his work and thus to view *Under Milk Wood*, as Daniel Jones suggested, as the result of a 'slow and *natural* process', a play which grew out of Dylan's temper and talents and experience.

General questions

1 Write short character sketches of (a) Captain Cat and (b) the Reverend Eli Jenkins.

Note-form guideline answer

(a) Introduction to each character – first appearance (or first sound, if you like) – general outline and definition of each – where living – function – importance of past and present.

(b) Detail on Captain Cat – 'retired blind sea captain' – range of his references – living in the past (quote 'Oh, my dead dears') – his listening – the detail of the children – the postman's round – the compensation for his blindness by his heightened sense of hearing – his delight in the knowledge of what everyone in the village is doing – his first long speech – his deductions (like the arrival of Polly Garter).

(c) Detail on his memories as he sleeps in the afternoon – say what they tell you about the kind of man he was – (some detail on Rosie Probert) – love-making – the mixed nautical imagery – perhaps derived from real figure – sentimental – wry sense of humour. Give your own general impression of the man from the verse, the language he uses.

(d) The Reverend Eli Jenkins – function in the play for voices – poems – faith – essential characteristics – daily service of his own – what does this reveal? – is his poetry original? – his knowledge and range of reference – his giving thanks for the fact that the Welsh are musical – his visiting – his prose work.

(e) His poems at sunset – his 'White Book' – his love of tradition and history – his 'pantheistic' views (define and quote) – his druidism – the fact that he is the last person to be heard in the play – is Dylan Thomas emphasizing his role by giving him this position (i.e. the final words which are a comment on life and particularly this life in a small community?).

(f) Stress the roles of each in the play – contrast briefly – who is the most convincing and why – what does each tell you of Dylan Thomas's own sympathies?

2 'The warmth of his personality, his zest in every kind of human oddity, his love for his fellow-men comes out in his last completed work, *Under Milk Wood*' (Fraser). Discuss and illustrate this statement.

3 'There is no moral strength in *Under Milk Wood*, but hence no compassion, and so no real drama' (Holbrook). Discuss.

4 In *Under Milk Wood* 'more than in any other prose work of his, he managed to combine his *prose-gift* for *humorous fantasy* based upon *realistic observation* with his *poetic gift* for a *piled-up richness* of *evocative language*' (Fraser). Discuss and illustrate this statement with particular reference to the italicized statements.

5 What is meant by saying that the movement of *Under Milk Wood* is *not dramatic* but *cyclical*?

6 'His prose works with the exception of *Under Milk Wood* throw little light on his poetry' (Fraser). Discuss.

7 One interpretation of Dylan Thomas's poem *Ballad of the Long-Legged Bait* is that it represents 'a typically Welsh struggle, between natural sensuality and Puritanism' (Olson). Do you find any evidence of this struggle in *Under Milk Wood*?

8 'In Dylan Thomas's *Under Milk Wood*, when a mode of seriousness is not taken from Joyce, it is a mimic of Eliot' (Holbrook). Discuss.

9 Write a critical appreciation of Dylan Thomas's realization of (a) the village, (b) the sea, as a presence in *Under Milk Wood*.

10 It has been said (by D. Holbrook) that *Under Milk Wood* is deficient in controlled movement: 'the overladen, breathless patter of word relish becomes, after a while, destructive of our ability to take things in clearly and exactly'. Do you agree?

11 Assess the success of the device of the First and Second Voices to give continuity to *Under Milk Wood*.

12 'It is on the flow of ebullient language that the play's appeal depends' (Holbrook). Has *Under Milk Wood* no other appeal?

13 '*Under Milk Wood* is trivial. And, indeed, it is really dangerous, because it flatters and reinforces the resistance to these developments we need. We need to be able to allow our tender feelings to flow – *Under Milk Wood* reinforces untenderness. It is a cruel work, inviting our cruel laughter. We need to understand love better – *Under Milk Wood* disguises and confuses. . . . All it may be said to have is comedy and linguistic exuberance. . . . As art it takes us nowhere, and merely flatters the suburban prejudices' (Holbrook). Examine each of these strictures in turn, indicating your own attitudes and responses.

14 Discuss the main poetic devices used by Dylan Thomas in his poems and *Under Milk Wood*.

15 Discuss the statement that *Under Milk Wood* lacks dramatic progression and is merely episodic reportage.

16 Write a general appreciation of the female characters of *Under Milk Wood*.

17 Write short character-sketches of (a) Mrs Ogmore-Pritchard, (b) Polly Garter.

18 Do you agree that *Under Milk Wood* lacks compassion?

19 'The most successful passages in *Under Milk Wood* are those where an amoral playful vigour is in order, and where the cruelty or solemnity of the child-spirit in Thomas is not maliciously drawn out, where he is not making a special plea for himself' (Holbrook). In your answer indicate the meaning which the word *amoral* has for you, by comparing it with *immoral* and *unmoral*.

20 Can you discern any 'religious' attitude in *Under Milk Wood*?

21 The prose-pieces contained in Dylan Thomas's *The Map of Love* have been characterized as having a semisurrealist flavour, relying on shock-tactics, cruelty and obscenity. Do you find examples of the latter in *Under Milk Wood*?

22 Do you agree that in *Under Milk Wood* Dylan Thomas invented a new literary form, turning the radio form of the 'feature' in literature?

23 'The characters are not confronted with choices; they behave according to their nature, mean, thriftless or generous, and are to be accepted, like natural objects, for being what they are' (Fraser). Discuss.

24 'Essentially *Under Milk Wood* is not a drama' (Holbrook). Discuss.

25 Discuss the view that *Under Milk Wood* is at its best when engaged in caricature removed from reality (e.g. Mrs Ogmore-Pritchard), and at its worst when it approaches real life and emotion (e.g. Polly Garter, the Cherry Owens, Captain Cat and Rosie Probert).

Further reading

1 Collected and selected works of Dylan Thomas

The World I Breathe

Selected Writings, Introduction by J. L. Sweeney

Collected Poems, 1934–1952

A Prospect of the Sea and Other Stories and Prose Writings, edited by D. Jones

The Letters of Dylan Thomas to Vernon Watkins

The Poems of Dylan Thomas, edited by Daniel Jones.

2 Separate works

18 Poems

Twenty-Five Poems

The Map of Love (Verse and Prose)

Portrait of the Artist as a Young Dog. Stories.

New Poems

Deaths and Entrances. Verse.

Twenty-Six Poems. A limited edition.

In Country Sleep. Six poems.

The Doctor and the Devils, from the story by Donald Taylor. Film scenario.

Under Milk Wood, A Play for Voices (1954). Published posthumously.

Quite Early One Morning (1954). Broadcasts

Adventures in the Skin Trade and Other Stories.

3 Critical and biographical studies

D. Stanford: *Dylan Thomas: A Literary Study*

E. Olson: *The Poetry of Dylan Thomas*

J. M. Brinnin: *Dylan Thomas in America*

David Daiches: *Literary Essays*

Thomas Parry: *A History of Welsh Poetry*

H. Treece: *Dylan Thomas: Dog Among the Fairies*

Caitlin Thomas: *Left-Over Life to Kill*

Caitlin Thomas: *Almost Posthumous Letter to My Daughter*

John Wain: *Preliminary Essays*

C. Brooke Rose: *A Grammar of Metaphor*

G. S. Fraser: *Dylan Thomas*

E. W. Tedlock: *Dylan Thomas: The Legend and the Poet*

W. Y. Tindall: *A Reader's Guide to Dylan Thomas*

T. H. Jones: *Dylan Thomas*

David Holbrook: 'Metaphor and Maturity: J. F. Powys and Dylan Thomas', in *The Pelican Guide to English Literature: The Modern Age*

David Holbrook: *Llareggub Revisited: Dylan Thomas and the State of Modern Poetry*

Douglas Cleverdon: *The Growth of Milk Wood*

Andrew Sinclair: *Dylan Thomas: Poet of His People*

Daniel Jones: *My Friend Dylan Thomas*

Paul Ferris: *Dylan Thomas*

Brodie's Notes

D. H. Lawrence	**The Rainbow**
D. H. Lawrence	**Sons and Lovers**
D. H. Lawrence	**Women in Love**
Harper Lee	**To Kill a Mockingbird**
Laurie Lee	**Cider with Rosie**
Christopher Marlowe	**Dr Faustus**
Arthur Miller	**The Crucible**
Arthur Miller	**Death of a Salesman**
John Milton	**Paradise Lost**
Robert C. O'Brien	**Z for Zachariah**
Sean O'Casey	**Juno and the Paycock**
George Orwell	**Animal Farm**
George Orwell	**1984**
J. B. Priestley	**An Inspector Calls**
J. D. Salinger	**The Catcher in the Rye**
William Shakespeare	**Antony and Cleopatra**
William Shakespeare	**As You Like It**
William Shakespeare	**Hamlet**
William Shakespeare	**Henry IV Part I**
William Shakespeare	**Julius Caesar**
William Shakespeare	**King Lear**
William Shakespeare	**Macbeth**
William Shakespeare	**Measure for Measure**
William Shakespeare	**The Merchant of Venice**
William Shakespeare	**A Midsummer Night's Dream**
William Shakespeare	**Much Ado about Nothing**
William Shakespeare	**Othello**
William Shakespeare	**Richard II**
William Shakespeare	**Romeo and Juliet**
William Shakespeare	**The Tempest**
William Shakespeare	**Twelfth Night**
George Bernard Shaw	**Pygmalion**
Alan Sillitoe	**Selected Fiction**
John Steinbeck	**Of Mice and Men** and **The Pearl**
Jonathan Swift	**Gulliver's Travels**
Dylan Thomas	**Under Milk Wood**
Alice Walker	**The Color Purple**
W. B. Yeats	**Selected Poetry**

ENGLISH COURSEWORK BOOKS

Terri Apter	**Women and Society**
Kevin Dowling	**Drama and Poetry**
Philip Gooden	**Conflict**
Philip Gooden	**Science Fiction**
Margaret K. Gray	**Modern Drama**
Graham Handley	**Modern Poetry**
Graham Handley	**Prose**
Graham Handley	**Childhood and Adolescence**
R. J. Sims	**The Short Story**